P U B   W
I N
Wiltshire

THIRTY CIRCULAR WALKS
AROUND WILTSHIRE INNS

Nick Channer

COUNTRYSIDE BOOKS
NEWBURY, BERKSHIRE

First Published 1993
© Nick Channer 1993

COUNTRYSIDE BOOKS
3 Catherine Road
Newbury, Berkshire

ISBN 1 85306 243 X

Designed by Mon Mohan
Cover illustration by Colin Doggett
Photographs by the Author
Maps drawn by Bob Carr

Produced through MRM Associates Ltd., Reading
Typeset by Paragon Typesetters, Queensferry, Clwyd
Printed in England

Contents

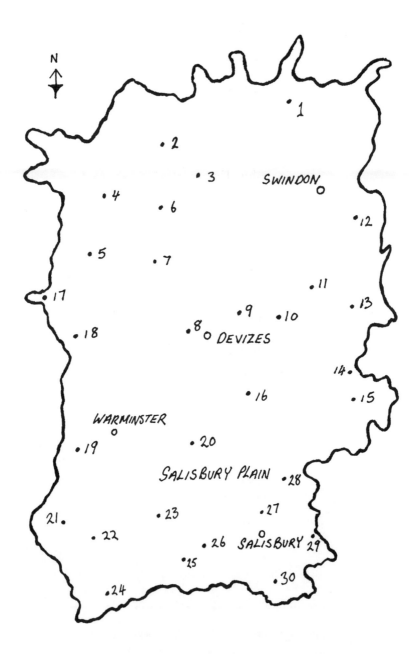

Area map showing locations of the walks.

Publisher's Note

We hope that you obtain considerable enjoyment from this book; great care has been taken in its preparation. However, changes of landlord and actual closures are sadly not uncommon. We are anxious that all details concerning both pubs and walks are kept as up to date as possible, and would therefore welcome information from readers which would be relevant to future editions.

Introduction

Being a real ale drinker and someone who has been known to visit the odd hostelry from time to time, I set out with delight on my task of combining 30 good pubs with 30 good walks in this area of infinite variety. I tend to think Wiltshire is underrated as a county. Perhaps too many people speed through it on their way to the West Country, eager to escape the congested environs of London and the pressure of modern day life, without fully appreciating its stark beauty and spacious landscapes. After the clutter of the Thames Valley and the home counties, these breathtaking Wessex downs inspire a sense of space and freedom as well as providing a window on our history.

Apart from the timeless prehistoric sites, the monoliths and barrows, the great houses and the sweeping chalk downlands, there are belts of richly-coloured woodland and forest, snug villages – many recorded in Saxon times – canals and mellow stone cottages, and undiscovered river valleys of more gentle beauty where there are still very few reminders of life in the late 20th century. Then there is the Ridgeway and a whole network of old drovers' roads and smugglers' routes. There is Salisbury Plain too – that enigmatic 300 square mile tract of land at the very heart of Wiltshire.

The pubs are, in the main, unspoilt traditional country inns – the kind supported and endorsed by CAMRA and deliberately not in keeping with the theme pub format – with a good range of real ales and a variety of wholesome pub fare to satisfy the hungry and the thirsty walker. Many are family-based pubs with good facilities for children. One or two are more basic, with a simple menu but a welcoming unpretentious air. A couple of them are slightly more upmarket restaurant pubs but even here, as with all of them, walkers and families are made most welcome.

With a choice of over 700 pubs in the county, selecting just 30 was a difficult task indeed. Many otherwise excellent establishments had to be excluded because a suitable walk could not be woven around them, or because they were too near other good pubs. However, I enjoyed all these inns and I would like to think that my favourable impressions coincide with yours.

To avoid repetition, I have omitted pub opening hours, so please assume the inn is open for business and serving food during the normal times unless otherwise stated. Out of courtesy, I would ask you please to mention to the landlord that you are intending to leave a car on the premises whilst you walk. In view of the undulating terrain on some of the described circuits, many people will want to do the walk prior to visiting the pub! Leaving a car at the inn for several hours should not present a problem as long as you visit the pub afterwards. I have sought the permission of each landlord to use his car park. You may find it easier to ring the pub in advance to check parking and book food. I have listed individual telephone numbers.

The walks I have featured are all circular and are based on rights of way. They are fairly undemanding and vary in length from 3 to 6 miles, and the sketch maps are designed to give a simple yet accurate idea of the route to be taken. For more detail I would urge you to carry the relevant Ordnance Survey sheet with you.

A word of warning about what to expect underfoot. In spring and summer these routes are a delight to walk. In dry conditions a good pair of shoes or boots should be sufficient. In winter something much sturdier will be necessary – particularly after prolonged periods of rain.

Having walked more than 100 miles of footpaths for this book, I hope that the results of my efforts characterize and reflect the diversity and true spirit of the county. I hope you agree and I wish you many hours of happy walking in the Wiltshire air.

Nick Channer
April 1993

① Castle Eaton
The Red Lion

Formerly a Courage house, the Red Lion is now owned by Ushers and has the distinction of being the first inn on the Thames – the river rises nearby. The beer garden slopes down to the willow-fringed Thames and in high summer this proves to be one of the pub's greatest attractions. Custom at this time of the year is also boosted by canoeists and cyclists, and walkers undertaking the Thames Path. During the rest of the year, the Red Lion's clientele comprises mostly local and passing trade. It is altogether quieter and more sedate at this time, as I found when I called one wet December afternoon.

Inside this graceful 18th century inn, built of red brick with a Cotswold stone tile roof, there are several bars – one being the villagers' snug or lounge bar with its cosy log fire in winter, black and white photographs of bygone village scenes, and part brick and stone walls, the other being the public bar. There is a restaurant but you can eat in the bar if you prefer. A blackboard offers a range of suggested winter and summer specialities. On Sunday there is a traditional roast, while the pub menu comprises toasted sandwiches, soup, duck pâté and other snacks. Main dishes include steak and kidney pie, Lincolnshire sausage, grilled 8 oz sirloin steak and grilled lemon sole.

Children and vegetarians are catered for. Among the real ales are Ushers Best and Founders Strong Ale, and there is usually a guest beer. Fosters, Hofmeister and Guinness are also available.

Another notable feature at the Red Lion, more a locally famous tradition, is the Pétanque Club which plays in the garden at the side. The game is similar to French boules. The tradition was originated by a previous landlord. The club has its own team but non members are welcome. Among the attractions for children is a cage containing eight chipmunks, situated at the rear of the pub.

Telephone: Cirencester (0285) 810280.

How to get there: Castle Eaton is in the north east corner of Wiltshire. From Swindon follow the A419 towards Cirencester and Gloucester. The turning to Castle Eaton is on the right and is signposted. On entering the village, bear left into The Street. The Red Lion is on the left.

Parking: There is usually plenty of room to park at the Red Lion. Alternatively, look for a space elsewhere in the village.

Length of the walk: 4 miles. Map: OS Landranger 163 Cheltenham and Cirencester (GR 145957).

Castle Eaton is one of the prettiest villages in the area − its charming, picturesque buildings clustered around a rectangle of streets. Old Father Thames is but a fledgling at this point, the shallow, infant river cutting a broad sweep around the back of the village. From the road bridge the river can be seen meandering alongside the gardens of private houses towards the church, with its Victorian bell turret and spire, over on the right bank. The walk follows level roads, field paths and tracks, across a pleasant rural landscape, skirting the perimeter of Fairford Airfield and the gardens of houses at neighbouring Marston Meysey.

The Walk

Leave the inn by turning right and then right again, signposted Kempsford and Fairford. Follow the road, crossing the bridge over the Thames. Continue along the road between fields. A quick glance around you reveals a flat landscape of fields and hedgerows. The scenery is different in appearance and character to mid and south Wiltshire, more reminiscent of the Cotswolds which lie only a few miles to the north.

At the junction bear right. Along this stretch the church tower at Kempsford is visible across the fields. Closer at hand, only a short distance away, is the church tower at Castle Eaton and near to it is the Red Lion with its garden sloping down to the river. At the T junction

9

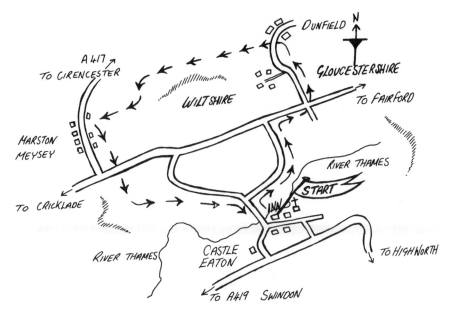

turn right, signposted Kempsford. After several minutes, bear left along the narrow lane to Dunfield. Pass a waymarked footpath on the left and keep on the lane. Half right, across the fields, are the buildings of Fairford Airfield. Ignore a turning to Orchard House, Poplar House and Cox's Farm, and continue.

On reaching the hamlet of Dunfield, bear left onto a waymarked path as the road veers right. Cross the stile and aim half right towards the hedgerow. Once over the next stile, go right, into the adjoining field, and then immediately left to follow the field boundary. After some minutes you join a grassy track running alongside the perimeter of Fairford Airfield. Go forward onto a path running through a tunnel of trees. Follow the path between the trees for some considerable distance. Eventually it bends sharp left, where there is a gate into a field on the right. Keep on the main path with thick woodland now on the right and on a line of trees on the left. Soon the path bears sharp right. Continue as it turns left again and then right. On reaching a drive serving a number of houses and bungalows, you have a choice.

To continue with the main walk, bear left along the drive. If you wish to look around the village of Marston Meysey, go forward along the drive to the road, where there are a number of pretty stone cottages, and then return to this point in order to resume the walk.

Follow the track as it runs along the back of the village, passing various houses and gardens. When it bears sharp left, proceed ahead along the field edge. Pass into the next field and continue to the road. On the opposite side join a track running to the right of some barns. When you reach the entrance to The Round House, a modern building of curious design, bear left over a stile. Join a track and bear right. Follow the track round a right and left bend. At the next bend go forward over a stile and join a path cutting between fields. Cross a ditch by means of a small footbridge and continue along the right hand edge of the field. Beyond the corner bear right into the adjacent field. Go slightly right along a vague path to the next boundary where a stile takes you out to the drive leading to a caravan park.

Cross the drive and enter the next field. Aim slightly left to a gate in the next boundary. Beyond the hedge proceed towards the wire fence and then head half right, making for its right hand corner. Walk towards the buildings of Castle Eaton, keeping the fence on your immediate left. On reaching the road, turn right and return to the Red Lion in the village centre. If time permits, however, it is worth extending the walk by a couple of hundred yards in order to visit the church. Walk along the road and when it bends right, turn left along a path beside farm buildings to reach the church. On leaving, return to the inn by the same route.

② Charlton
The Horse and Groom

The Horse and Groom is a Grade II listed 300 year old Cotswold stone inn. It has been part of the Suffolk estate in that time, and is now a freehouse. The inn comprises several bars including the lounge bar and the Charlton bar, as well as a more intimate area for dining. There is an inglenook fireplace and photographs of hunting scenes and vintage cars.

The food is freshly prepared and includes stilton and mushroom pasta, chicken and beef curry and vegetarian's platter. There are also baps with fillings including egg mayonnaise, prawn and garlic, and cream cheese and salad. The inn is closed on Mondays, and on Sunday evenings in January, February and March. Food is available throughout both sessions when the inn is open. There is a good range of real ales from the handpump. They include Wadworth 6X, Mole's Bitter and Archers Village Bitter. Lagers include Pils, Double Diamond and Carlsberg. There is also Bland's Draught Cider. Children over 14 are welcome. Dogs may join you in the public bar. There is a garden and a play area.

Telephone: Malmesbury (0666) 823904.

How to get there: Charlton is a couple of miles to the north of Malmesbury, on the B4040 Cricklade road. Coming from Malmesbury, go right through the village until you reach the Horse and Groom on the left.

Parking: There is room to park at the inn. Otherwise look for a space along the road leading to Charlton Park. There is usually room outside the church, near the main gates into Charlton Park.

Length of the walk: 4 miles. Map: OS Landranger 173 Swindon and Devizes (GR 966889).

This is a delightful ramble in the scenic country near Malmesbury. In the main, the circuit follows bridleways which can become very wet after heavy rain, so high summer or a dry crisp autumn is an ideal time to undertake it. During its middle stages the walk provides good views over to the village of Hankerton. On the return leg there are splendid glimpses of Charlton Park in the distance.

The Walk
From the pub car park bear left and go down the road to the left turning (signposted 'Hankerton'). Follow the lane towards the village, between various houses and cottages. Pass Perry Green Cottage and head out of Charlton. Now, the road cuts between fields and hedgerows. Just before the lane bends quite sharply to the right, there is a waymarked bridleway crossing the route of the road. Turn right, go through the gate and follow the bridleway along the field edge. Keep to the track, following it along several field boundaries. There are good views over some pretty, undulating farmland with a network of fields divided up by hedgerows and trees.

On reaching the edge of woodland, where there are two gates, go through the gate on the right and continue ahead along the field edge with trees on your left. In the corner swing right and then left through the gate. Follow the field edge, with woodland still on the left. Over to the right there is a very pleasant view of rolling, partly wooded scenery. Pass through a gate into the next field, with pretty woodland over to the right. Make your way up the field, keeping the trees still on your left. Further up go through a wooden gate on the left and then bear right along waymarked bridleway between fields and fences. The bridleway curves left and there is woodland on the right and fields on the left. Further on, if you look over to the left, you can see the church tower at Hankerton. Nearer to hand, across the fields, are the houses of Bullock's Horn.

When you reach a metalled lane, turn left and follow it between trees and hedgerows. In a minute or two, you come to Bullock's Horn,

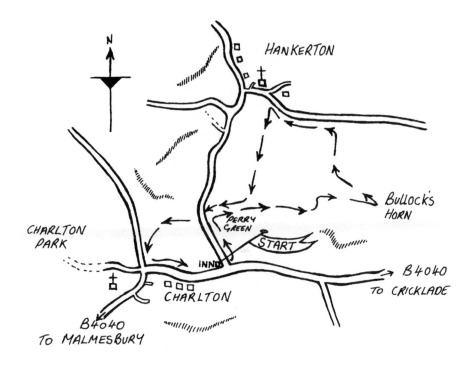

where a cluster of houses stands guard over a small pond and some trees. Proceed ahead towards April Cottage, joining a bridleway to the right of it. Follow it as it runs alongside the garden of the cottage. Go through a gate and then follow the bridleway along the right edge of the field. Up ahead, on the southern fringes of the Cotswolds, is the village of Hankerton, with the church rising above the rooftops.

On reaching a track on the right, join it and follow it to the road. Turn left and walk along the lane towards Hankerton. After several minutes pass a row of bungalows on the right. The road begins to curve to the right and here there is a good view of Hankerton church. Opposite Old Farm Close take the footpath signposted to Andover's Gorse. Go through the gate and then slightly left to the gate in the next boundary. Once through the gate turn right and follow the field edge, keeping the hedgerow on the right. In the top right corner, pass into the next field and continue. After about 75 yards bear right through an opening into the adjoining field, then follow the left boundary, with the hedge on the left. Go as far as the field corner, cross over the little ditch and then the stile. Proceed ahead across the field. When you reach the bridleway, recognisable from the earlier part of this walk, turn right and retrace your steps back to the road.

Cross over, go through the gap into the field and bear right along the bridleway. Complete three sides of the field and then look for a blue bridleway waymarker. Cross into the adjacent right hand field, through the opening. Follow the left boundary. Over to the right is the graceful outline of Charlton Park, the great house standing in imposing isolation among the trees. This magnificent 17th century Grade I listed building was the home of the Earls of Suffolk and Berkshire between 1607 and 1939. There are claims that Lord Berkshire fathered an illegitimate daughter who was supposedly born here. When she grew up, Mary Davis became one of Charles II's mistresses until Nell Gwyn, realising she had a rival for the King's affections, fed her jalap, a purgative drug. It was here too that John Dryden, the poet and playwright, took refuge during the Great Plague and the Fire of London. He wrote his 'Annus Mirabilis' here, an account in verse of the Dutch War and the Great Fire. Charlton Park, once a school, stood empty for 25 years and was under threat of demolition until eventually, in the mid 1970s, it was painstakingly restored and converted into luxury apartments.

Follow the field edge until you reach a stile and gap, taking you onto Charlton playing fields and sports area. Aim half right, making for the point at which a wall and hedge meet. Pass through the gap and out to the road. Turn left and make for the centre of Charlton. The village church of St John the Baptist, over to the right, has strong associations with Charlton Park. Inside, there is an effigy of Sir Henry Knyvett and his family. Sir Henry, owner of the original house, died in 1598. It was one of his daughters who married the first Earl of Suffolk and inherited the estate. Some time after Sir Henry's death, the earlier building was refashioned into the much larger mansion you see today. The village itself was once populated by estate workers from Charlton Park. In recent years there has been much new building in Charlton, using various types of bradstone. The effect is quite complementary, helping to unify what is essentially a Cotswold village.

At the main junction head towards Cricklade. Walk along the street, keeping to the pavement. Soon you are back at the car park of the Horse and Groom.

3 Brinkworth
The Suffolk Arms

The Suffolk Arms is about 150 years old. Apparently it was once a house of ill-repute, but these days there is nothing sordid about its reputation! Its name originates from the Suffolk estate which once stretched for miles in this area. The inn is on the edge of Brinkworth and from the bar there are glorious views over rolling countryside to the south. The clientele is largely local, though the pub attracts a good deal of passing trade. It is especially popular with walkers and is a simple straightforward inn with a friendly welcoming atmosphere. The single bar has beams, brass plates, horse brasses, horse shoes, wall lights and table lamps. There is a cosy log fire in winter. The inn also has a games area, including a dartboard and pool table. There is also a juke box and fruit machine.

The menu caters for most tastes, with soup of the day, various steaks, lasagne, a wide variety of homemade pies – very much a speciality here – deep fried chicken, jacket potatoes, sandwiches and toasties. There is also a range of desserts and a children's menu. Real ales include Wadworth 6X, Archers Village Bitter, which is traditionally brewed in Swindon, and Ruddles Best Bitter. There is Triple Crown and Courage Best on keg, and Guinness, Fosters and Strongbow Dry Cider are also available.

At the rear of the inn is a beer garden with a play area for children and toddlers. No dogs please. There is also a barbecue area where inn food is cooked. Alternatively, you can bring your own and have it barbecued.
Telephone: Malmesbury (0666) 510436.

How to get there: Brinkworth straddles the B4042 road and is situated between Wootton Bassett and Malmesbury, a couple of miles due north of the M4. The Suffolk Arms is east of the village centre, on the main road.

Parking: There is a car park at the rear of the Suffolk Arms. Limited parking may be possible in the vicinity of the church. School Hill, next to the Three Crowns, is quieter than the main village street and therefore easier. If you park here, take the path north of the B4042 (near the church) thus avoiding lengthy road walking, and link up with the main walk, where a sign on a gate asks you to keep dogs on a lead.

Length of the walk: 3½ miles. Map: OS Landranger 173 Swindon and Devizes (GR 028852).

Brinkworth is a straggling linear village, not especially attractive but set impressively in the gently rolling hills of north Wiltshire. John Betjeman included the church in his famous 'Parish Churches', along with the nearby Somerfords and Dauntsey – all of them, to quote Betjeman, surely 'worth bicycling twelve miles against the wind to see.'

From the higher ground of this walk there are excellent views over a network of undulating fields, creating a harmonious rural picture that has a strong Cotswold hint about it. It is particularly well-waymarked and follows a number of field paths, bridleways and byways. There are a great many stiles on the outward leg!

The Walk
From the car park turn right along the B4042 for a few yards, then bear right to join a 'No through road'. Follow it for about 200 yards, with a line of telegraph poles on the left. Look for a stile in the left boundary and cross into the field, then through the gateway into the next field. Join a green lane running between trees and hedges, following it to the road. Turn right for a few steps and then left to join a waymarked bridleway.

Follow the path between hedgerows and trees. There are delightful views over to the right along this stretch. Note a dilapidated old cow shed in the field on the right. At the bend follow the bridle path round to the left. On reaching a track opposite a cottage, turn right and here there is an impressive view of a green and rolling landscape. Go down

17

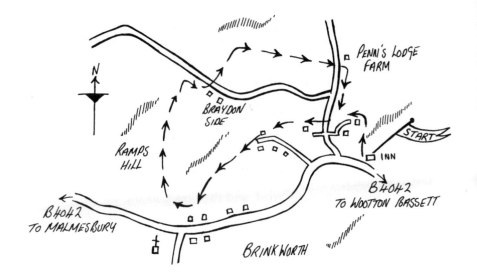

the track passing some cottages and then through several gates. Follow
the byway between hedges and further on go through a wooden gate
to join a path between banks of scrub and trees. Pass through another
wooden gate and out onto a broad grassy ride running between
hedges. Brinkworth church is visible a little to the left.

After a couple of minutes you reach a gate which leads you out to
another byway. Turn right for a few yards along the broad path until
you reach a gate on the right. There is a sign: 'Please keep your dogs
on a lead'. Go through the gate and head across the field, passing over
a stream and on up the hillside towards the next boundary. Cross
another stile and continue up the hill. Pause on occasions to look back
over a rolling landscape towards Brinkworth and, beyond it, the hilly,
semi-wooded countryside around RAF Lyneham. Keep the hedgerow
a few yards away to your left. On reaching another stile go into the
next field and down the hill to the boundary where there is a stile.
Cross it, followed by another stile and a footbridge. Proceed up the
field edge with the hedge on the immediate right. In the corner cross
into another field. The farm buildings at Braydon Side are clearly seen
now. Go forward into the next field via the stile and footbridge.

Follow the direction of the waymarker by heading across the field
to the far corner where a gate leads you out to the road. Turn right
and go up the lane towards the farm buildings. Beyond them bear left
onto a bridleway (at the second of two gates). Follow the field
boundary and eventually you reach the corner. Pass through a gate to
join another bridleway. Turn right and keep to the bridlepath along

18

the edge of the field. Over to the left are the trees of Somerford Common. To the right, at intervals, are good views of Brinkworth and on the distant horizon the hazy outline of Brinkworth church. Further on, join a clear track and aim for some farm buildings up ahead. Go through a gate and out to the road opposite Penn's Lodge Farm. Bear right and keep on the road passing an assortment of houses and bungalows. Follow the road down into the dip and pass a turning on the right to Braydon Side.

Begin the upward pull, making for the outskirts of Brinkworth. Just beyond a cottage called Poacher's Pocket you pass the waymarked bridlepath from earlier in the walk. Continue along the road for a short distance. Bear left before a bungalow and retrace your steps across the fields to the 'no through road' and then back to the car park at the Suffolk Arms.

Castle Combe
The White Hart

The White Hart, half-timbered beneath its bright whitened exterior, appeals to both tourists and village locals and is always deservedly busy. In the summer it is visitors to this most popular of English villages who swell the numbers. Inside, it comprises a flagstoned main bar and a family room. There are many attractive features to be seen, and low ceilings, beams and a cosy log fire in winter add to the inn's charm. There is also a pleasant beer garden and a sheltered courtyard at the back of the pub.

The choice of food at the White Hart is extensive and includes ploughman's lunches (ham, brie, cheddar and stilton), homemade cottage pie, Cumberland sausages, ham, egg and chips, bacon, lettuce and tomato roll, chilli con carne, deep fried scampi and jumbo sausage. There is also a range of jacket potatoes, sirloin steak, homemade soup, lasagne, curry (chicken or beef). If none of these dishes appeal, you can look at the daily specials board. On Sunday there is a traditional roast. Among the real ales from the handpump are Wadworth 6X, Butcombe, Bass and Ruddles County. There is also Scrumpy Jack Strong Cider.

Telephone: Castle Combe (0249) 782295.

How to get there: From Chippenham take the A420 west of the town and then join the B4039. Turn left beyond the motor racing circuit and follow the road down into Castle Combe village centre. From the west follow the A420 and turn left at Ford for Castle Combe.

Parking: The White Hart does not have a car park. There are, however, spaces for a few cars outside the inn, but bear in mind that in spring and summer Castle Combe is usually very busy. There is a car park about ½ mile from the pub at Upper Castle Combe. Turn right out of the car park and follow the road down through the village.

Length of the walk: 3½ miles. Map: OS Landranger 173 Swindon and Devizes (GR 843772).

Despite its isolated position in a wooded hollow, away from busy main roads and urban intrusion, Castle Combe is one of the most visited sites in the country. The village is like something from a child's picture book — hence the decision by film-makers to use it as the setting for 'Doctor Doolittle' in the mid 1960s. Voted the prettiest village in England in 1962, Castle Combe has all the ingredients to make it a tourist's dream: a market cross, a fast-flowing stream in the main street, a medieval packhorse bridge and the remains of a Norman castle. The village was once a prosperous centre of the wood trade, and became famous for its distinctive red and white cloth.

This ramble explores the delightful undiscovered countryside to the south of Castle Combe. Apart from two settlements, Ford and Long Dean, and the odd, brief stretch of road, the route strenuously avoids obvious reminders of the 20th century by keeping to timeless valleys and tumbling wooded hillsides. Here and there, the walk runs parallel with the By Brook, a tributary of the Avon. There are several steepish climbs but hopefully nothing too taxing! Be prepared for crowds in Castle Combe during the summer. Weekends are also busy.

The Walk
From the front of The White Hart, turn left and walk down between lines of charming cottages with stone tiled roofs. Pass over the By Brook. At this point there is the classic view of Castle Combe reproduced in thousands of photographs, postcards, calendars and the like. Follow the road with the brook running beside it. As the road begins to climb up through the trees, veer right to join a waymarked path running up the bank into the woods. The path climbs steeply between the trees. Eventually, it levels out and cuts between banks of bushes, gorse and scrub. It winds for some time over the higher ground, at length reaching the road.

Turn left here and when you reach the junction, go forward for several yards and then bear right through a gate. Turn immediately

21

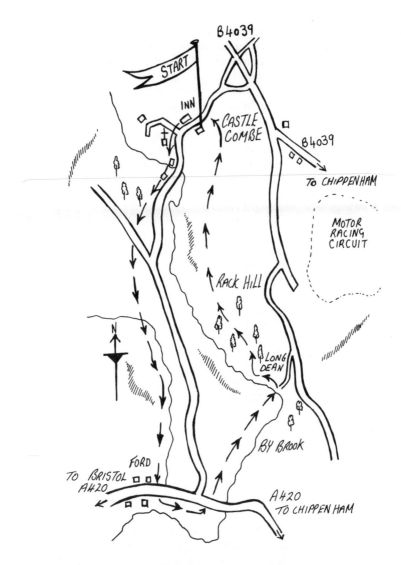

left, signposted 'Ford 1 mile'. Follow the clear path through the trees. The ground on the right falls away to reveal a charming wooded dell. Cross a stile, emerging now onto high open ground. There are good views from here down to the valley. Keep to the path as it traverses the upper slopes. When you reach a solitary wooden waymarker, veer half right and descend the hillside to the wooded corner. Look for a path threading through the trees and running down to the water. Cross the brook by means of a dilapidated old footbridge which can become waterlogged after heavy rain. Cross the stile into the field and continue ahead with woodland on the right. In the corner, follow a path running alongside the brook. If the going is difficult here, an alternative path has been fashioned along the right bank, rejoining the main path further on.

As you approach the boundaries of a small bungalow, swing right into the adjoining field. Leave the field at the little stile and go down the lane, passing various houses and cottages, to the main road in the village of Ford. Turn left along the road for a few yards, then left again to join the Castle Combe road. Follow this between banks of trees and when it swings left, bear right onto a waymarked path to Long Dean. The path traces a vague but visible line across the slopes of the hillside. There are good views of the By Brook in the valley below. Join a clear path and continue ahead. Go through a wooden gate and follow a sunken path down to the lane, almost at Long Dean. Note the sluice gate across the grass beyond the mill. Pass over the By Brook and progress between a number of charming stone cottages. This is Long Dean, a peaceful hamlet in an idyllic setting possibly even more remote and secluded than Castle Combe. Undoubtedly, it is less crowded, being off the tourist trail.

On reaching a junction with a letter box set in the wall, turn left and follow the track past Rose Cottage and up the hill between fields, hedgerows and trees. When the track veers left to a gate, continue ahead up a green lane towards Rack Hill. Go through a stile and continue over the hill and down the clear path, following a route between trees and light woodland. Just beyond a footpath sign on the right, take a grassy path swinging half right. This climbs quite steeply to a stile beside the remains of some old stone gate pillars. Continue through an area of woodland with clumps of brambles either side of you. Further on, the path levels out and runs in a straight line between the trees, with splendid views on the left of Castle Combe nestling in the hollow.

Later on, the path hugs the edge of a field. Follow it round a right hand bend and continue through the trees. When you reach a junction of paths, with a field opposite, bear left and drop down the sunken path to emerge at the roadside opposite a cottage. Turn left and return to the centre of Castle Combe.

5 Box Hill
The Quarryman's Arms

The Quarryman's Arms is hidden away on a hillside above the village of Box. Its position is so out of the way that it's amazing anyone can find it. But find it they most certainly do, and it is particularly popular with walkers and cyclists. Hardly surprising, as the place has a distinctive but genuine atmosphere. The inn is an unusual split level building. From the outside it looks very small, rather reminiscent of an old fashioned railway station in the days of steam. Inside, it is spacious. In the heyday of the stone industry it became a favourite haunt of quarrymen who worked the quarries in the area. There are maps on the walls showing the location of the mines, and photographs of various local mining characters. The little snug, situated on the right as you come in, used to be the candlemaker's shop. If you are planning to eat here, then try and get a table by the window. The views over the surrounding countryside are stunning. The final leg of the walk described in this chapter can be seen from here.

The inn offers a wide selection of homecooked food. Starters include soup of the day and prawn cocktail. Main dishes include local trout, T-bone steak, 10 oz Wiltshire gammon, homemade quarryman's chicken, and broccoli and ham bake. There are ploughman's lunches,

large rolls and sandwiches and various specials. A 'kiddies' corner' includes fish fingers, chicken nuggets and the Box Hill Banger. Wadworth 6X, Oakhill, Badger and Butcombe Bitter are among the real ales on handpump. There are several guest ales too. Children and dogs are welcome, but the garden facilities are limited.
Telephone: Box (0225) 743569.

How to get there: Box Hill is immediately to the south of the A4, between Corsham and Bath. From Corsham bear left beyond the Rudlow Park Hotel into Hedgesparrow Lane, then go into Barnetts Hill and right at the junction. The inn is on the right. From Bath and Box turn right into Beech Road, then right at Barnetts Hill.

Parking: There is room to park at the inn. Limited room to park generally in Box Hill.

Length of the walk: 4 miles. Map: OS Landranger 173 Swindon and Devizes (GR 834693).

There is a great deal of variety on this delightful hilly walk located in an area renowned for its stone quarries. There is a flavour of the Cotswolds about it, even a hint of the Derbyshire Dales, with its rolling fields, glorious woodland, drystone walls and stone cottages. The walk makes for the village of Box, where there are splendid views of Brunel's Box Tunnel. The last part of the walk follows the banks of the pretty By Brook.

The Walk
From the front of the inn join a waymarked track opposite and follow it past the Old Post Office on the left. When the track reaches a T junction, go forward onto a grassy bank and veer left. Follow the line of the path across the grass to enter the trees. When you reach another junction, turn right and follow the path to the road. Bear right and go down to the road junction. Turn right into Boxfields Road. Follow the road between the trees and then veer left to join a waymarked path cutting across the field. When you reach a drystone wall, bear left and follow the path with the wall on your right. After a couple of minutes, swing right, through a gap in the wall, and follow the path towards a line of trees on the far side of the field.
   On reaching a track, turn right and follow it as it bends left passing between borders of ornamental trees and shrubs. Pass the main entrance to Hazelbury Manor on the right and continue beyond the pond. At this point swing left as the track heads towards open fields. Follow the path down the slope between shrubs and bushes and lines of trees. Pass several ponds on the left and right. At the point where

25

a bridleway crosses our route, go through the stile in front of you and descend the grassy slopes. This part of the walk is a scenic delight, particularly in summer. The semi-wooded slopes offer a network of paths to delight the walker.

Follow the path as it veers to the right of the lake and enters an area of thickish woodland. You are now on a wide bridleway (usually wet and muddy after rain). Ignore a left hand turning and continue on the main bridleway through the woods. Eventually you reach a stile. Go over it and down a track between trees to the road. Turn left on a sharp bend and go up the lane to the junction. Bear right and follow the road, beside some houses. At the junction join the A365 and follow its pavement into the centre of Box. There are good views on the right, across the village. Pass Chapel Lane. At the next junction bear sharp right to join the A4. Pass Bayly's Inn, from which Cromwell barred the local parson on the grounds 'he is an ignorant and scandalous minister profaning the Sabbath'. Just beyond the inn turn sharp left into Church Lane. Follow the lane, passing to the right of the church. At the far end of the lane bear right by Box House Cottage, going down the waymarked path between walls and pass over a pretty stream further down. By taking a few steps to the right to a gate you will be treated to a delightful prospect, as here the stream cascades charmingly down beneath the trees.

Resuming the walk, cross the bridge over the By Brook and at the junction go forward and straight up towards the left hand edge of the trees. Aim for a stile and a gateway beside the trees and continue over the next field. Glancing back at this stage, there are superb views back towards the village of Box nestling in the valley below. Away to the west, you can spot traffic zipping along the A4. Further up the hillside there is an impressive view of Box Tunnel on the right. Its scale and the classical design of its entrance make it one of Brunel's greatest engineeering achievements. It is over 3,000 yards long and was officially opened in 1841. At the time, it was the longest railway tunnel in the world and at one stage there were 4,000 men working on its construction. According to legend, the sun shines through the tunnel on Brunel's birthday in April. At this stage of the route you are walking above a shorter section of tunnel as the line once more cuts through the hillside. The graceful stone parapet above the mouth of the tunnel is just a few yards away to the right of the path.

Continue up the slope to the stile, cross it and proceed over the high ground towards the farm. Go through the gate towards the farm buildings and out to the road. Turn right and follow the road for a few yards until it bends left. Bear right here through a gate and then go across the field to the gate in the next boundary. From the path there are excellent views down to Box and up to Box Hill, with the

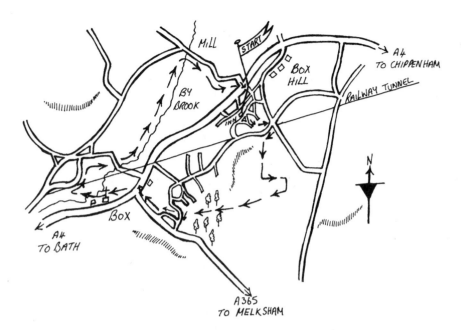

Quarryman's Arms nestling among the cottages.

Pass through the gate and descend the hillside to join the road. Cross over the By Brook and then bear immediately left to join a waterside path. Go over the footbridge and turn right. Note the spectacular sluice gate and the racing foaming water over to the right. Follow the clear path over another bridge and when you reach a stile on the left, leave the path and enter the field. Proceed ahead across the watermeadows, running parallel with the By Brook. In the next boundary pass through the gap into the next field and continue ahead. In the next hedge, with the brook now some way over to the right, go through a gap and follow the right boundary of the field until you exit into the lane. Turn right and after a short distance bear right where a sign says 'unsuitable for motors'. Cross By Brook and go between the buildings of the mill. Follow the lane as it rises quite steeply between hedgerows and banks. A backward glance reveals good views of Colerne, a neighbouring village on the horizon. The church stands out proudly on the hilltop. The control tower at the adjacent airfield is also visible. Colerne was an RAF station until its closure in the mid 1970s.

Eventually, after a stiff climb, you reach the main A4. Cross it to join Hedgesparrow Lane. After about 50 yards, at the junction, join Barnetts Hill and follow the road to the inn car park.

6 Sutton Benger
The Wellesley Arms

The Wellesley Arms is a solid old inn on the edge of this stone-belt village. The pub, which is a Wadworth House, is named after Arthur Wellesley, better known to us as His Grace the Duke of Wellington. It is thought Wellington stayed in the area on occasions and went hunting with the Duke of Beaufort. The precise age of the building is not known. The lounge bar is cosy and intimate with a mixture of tables, formal hardback chairs and comfortable armchairs. There are exposed beams and part stone walls, giving the bar a warm ambience and on the walls are various paintings and drawings of the Wellesley Arms.

Real ales extend to Wadworth 6X and traditional draught IPA. There is also Castlemaine XXXX, Stella Artois, Dry Blackthorn Cider, Guinness and Northgate Bitter. There is a separate dining room (not a restaurant – the landlord prefers it that way!), for which booking is necessary, but you can eat in the bar if you prefer. The menu is extensive and includes a number of specialities – steak and kidney pie, chicken, leek and stilton pie, and beef in Guinness casserole among them. The menu also includes sandwiches, several starters such as homemade soup and seafood cocktail, a range of grills including gammon and T bone steaks, vegetarian dishes, basket meals, salad dishes and jacket potatoes. There is a range of puddings including banana split, Mississippi mud pie and the intriguingly named Wicked Wellesley – this consists of meringue with chocolate ice cream, Tia Maria, cream and chocolate sauce (mouthwatering!). A traditional Sunday roast is included in the menu. Children and walkers are welcome, but dogs are confined to the public bar. For the music lover and the sporting enthusiast, the public bar includes a pool table, dartboard, quiz machine and juke box. There is also a garden at the rear of the inn.

Telephone: Chippenham (0249) 720251.

How to get there: Sutton Benger lies to the south of the M4. From junction 17 of the motorway, take the B4122 and at the junction bear left to join the B4069. The inn is on the left as you enter the village.

Parking: There is a car park for patrons to the rear of the Wellesley Arms. It is not advisable to park for any length of time at the side of the B4069. However, there is restricted parking in some of the adjacent side roads.

Length of the walk: 3 miles. Map: OS Landranger 173 Swindon and Devizes (GR 943786).

Sutton Benger is a very pleasant starting point for this short, undemanding walk. The population of this village was more than doubled in the 1970s when several new developments extended its boundaries. However, Sutton Benger still largely retains the character of an original Wiltshire village, particularly in the vicinity of the main street and the church. Beyond the village, the walk reaches the river Avon before crossing riverside fields and watermeadows within sight of the church at Christian Malford, standing in a prominent position on a bluff above the river.

The Walk
From the Wellesley Arms car park bear left and walk along the main B4069 Lyneham road. After a few yards, turn right into Chestnut Road. Follow the road until you reach Queens Close on the right. Note the waymarker post. Sutton Benger primary school is now on your left. At the far end of the cul-de-sac, take the narrow path cutting between two houses. On reaching the field, go forward to the gap in the next field boundary. Over on the easterly horizon Melsome Wood rises above the fields. In the skies above the wood, Hercules transport planes wheel almost noiselessly in and out of RAF Lyneham. Cross over a narrow ditch running along the boundary and bear left along the field edge towards a cottage. Just beyond it pass through a gap and

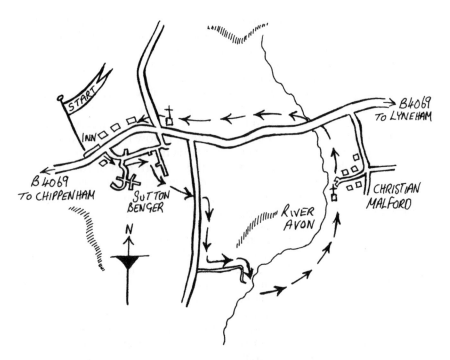

out to the road. Turn right. After about ½ mile, having passed beneath a line of electricity pylons, bear left onto a waymarked track. Follow it between hedges.

In due course the track swings sharp right and runs beside the river Avon on your left. Further on, you cross over the river beside the sluice gate. The scene here is quite striking, with the Avon flowing between fields and banks of scrub and the water boiling and churning beneath the bridge. Beyond the bridge, you leave the river to follow a grassy bridleway between hedges. As you approach the railway arch, with a gate in front of it, bear left through a gate into a field and follow the edge of it, with a belt of light woodland on the right.

Further on, join a grassy track running alongside some old farm buildings. After a few yards turn left through another gate into the field. Bear right and go into the next field. Aim now for the church at Christian Malford, clearly visible just up ahead across the fields. Its charming setting is one of the highlights of this walk. On reaching the field boundary, cross a footbridge into the next field and go straight ahead towards the church. Over on the left the Avon can be seen meandering through the countryside. The village of Sutton Benger is easily spotted beyond the river.

30

Cross the stile into the churchyard and continue forward to the road. Ignore Coronation Close on the left and proceed ahead for a few yards as far as the left hand footpath signposted 'Avon Weir ¾ mile'. To look round the village of Christian Malford, walk along the road between the buildings and then return to this point.

Take the path pointing to Avon Weir and follow it over the stile in the next boundary. Continue ahead. In the distance are the houses of Christian Malford. Aim for the stiles in the next boundary, with a footbridge between them. Once over them, follow the field edge with a high hedge on the right, heading towards the houses. At the hedge corner veer slightly left and make for the western end of the houses. Look for a tiny gap in the fence and hedgerow, near the last house. This provides access onto a narrow path taking you to a kissing gate and out to the road. On the opposite side of the road is the Christian Malford United Reform church.

Turn left and walk along the verge of the B4069 in a westerly direction. After a few yards you cross the river Avon. The river is quite wide at this point and there are good views once more of the church at Christian Malford. Immediately over the bridge, cross a stile on the right and then walk down the field, keeping roughly parallel with the road and passing under the pylons. Cross another stile in the next boundary and continue ahead. Follow a vague path across the field towards the houses of Sutton Benger. The path runs up alongside a hedgerow and a line of telegraph poles. Join a track on the outskirts of the village and when it bends left, continue forward over a stile into a paddock. Go forward to the right corner of the field and emerge into the road beside the Vintage Inn. This building has an unusual history, being at one time a chocolate factory, then a wine cellar.

Turn left and walk down to the junction opposite the Bell House Hotel. On the left here is the entrance to the church. Bear right and follow the main street of Sutton Benger as far as the car park of the Wellesley Arms, which will be found on the right.

⑦ Lacock
The George Inn

The George is one of the oldest buildings in Lacock. It dates from 1361 and has always been a public house. The face of George II is depicted on the pub sign. There are many attractive features inside, among them a medieval fireplace, a low beamed ceiling, mullioned windows, various upright timbers, flagstones and interconnecting bars. The log fire has a famous old treadwheel by which a dog would drive the turnspit. There are sketches available depicting the dog at work with the caption underneath: 'Does your grill provide such delicate control?'

There is a good range of food, including various homemade specials from the chalkboard, with steak and kidney pie, harvester pie and lasagne among them. From the menu you can choose a starter such as fruit juice or homemade soup of the day. The main dishes include T-bone steak, sirloin steak in various sauces including cream of stilton, brandy, cream and garlic, and red wine. There is also a choice of fish and poultry and a range of sandwiches and ploughman's lunches. Sweets include banana and toffee crunch and chocolate fudge cake. A children's corner offers sausage, chips and beans, and fish fingers, chips and beans. On Sunday there is a traditional roast. Real ales from the handpump are Wadworth 6X, IPA and Farmer's Glory, and Dry

Blackthorn Cider, Scrumpy Jack and Carlsberg are also served. Children and dogs are welcome and will enjoy the beer garden and play area at the rear of the inn. Accommodation for a longer stay is available at the landlord's farmhouse nearby. The George is a popular pub and can get very busy at weekends and on bank holidays. Telephone: Chippenham (0249) 730263.

How to get there: Lacock is just off the A350 Melksham to Chippenham road. Approaching from either direction, it is clearly signposted. The George is located in West Street in the village centre.

Parking: There is a car park at the rear of the inn. The village centre has some spaces and there is a large car park on the edge of Lacock to cope with the busy summer weekends.

Length of the walk: 4½ miles. Map: OS Landranger 173 Swindon and Devizes (GR 915686).

Lacock is one of Wiltshire's loveliest villages, a perfect example of medieval England. Its ancient streets are packed with tourists from home and abroad in summer, but during the winter, the village demonstrates a calmer, more dignified air. Out of season is therefore the ideal time to stroll in your own space, admiring the old timber buildings and gabled roofs. Be warned! You can spend a great deal of time in Lacock without even realising it. The walk crosses the Avon and climbs up above the village, passing through the estate of Bowden Park. There are superb views from this high ground over the surrounding countryside. The walk returns to Lacock by way of the watermeadows. The beautiful abbey can easily be seen across the river.

The Walk
Leave the inn by turning left and follow the road out of the village almost as far as the junction with the main A350. As you approach the junction bear right, signposted 'Reybridge ½ mile'. Follow the lane down between hedgerows, with views towards Naish Hill and Bowden Park. Keep to the lane as it curves left beside some cottages. Turn right, crossing the Avon by the stone road bridge, then bear left into the field. Aim for the little stile in the right hand boundary, at the point where the wall and the fence meet.

Cross over the lane to a path and follow it between fences and hedges. At the end of the path go into the field and veer right. Pass into the next field and then bear left, heading out across the field and aiming slightly right towards the gap in the far boundary hedge. Once through the gap, turn right and walk to the road. Veer left and head down the road avoiding the turning to the right. Follow the lane as it makes a gradual ascent. Further up, the road becomes noticeably

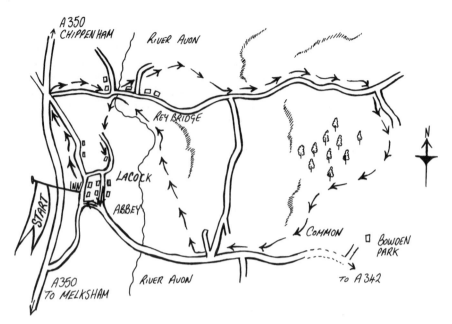

steeper. When it swings right, there is an opportunity to admire the splendid view from a field gateway. From here you can look west across a vast agricultural plain towards Bath and the Wiltshire/Avon border.

Go on up the lane past some farm buildings. As the road veers left cross a stile on the right and then bear left along the top of the fields. Keep the fence close by you on the left. When you reach a wood, cross a stile to join a path running between the trees and clumps of brambles. The path curves right and drops down gently to a stile. Proceed ahead along the field edge and keep the woodland on the right. Cross the stile on the right and aim obliquely left down through the parkland. There are magnificent views ahead over west Wiltshire. Nearer to hand is the graceful outline of Bowden Park. The house is late 18th century and was built for a wealthy Bristol merchant.

Make for the gap down between the two belts of woodland and on reaching it, head for the right hand corner where there is a stile. Descend the gentle slopes, pass over a crosstrack and go straight down the middle of the field with trees over to the left and the right. As you draw level with a cottage on the left, bear left towards it and make for the stile to the left of it. Go down the rough track, joining a clearer lane further on. Walk along the lane across the open ground of Bewley Common, owned by the National Trust.

34

Pass an imposing gateway guarded by two gatehouses. Turn right here and head down to the road at Bewley Common. Bear right and follow the road, shortly passing the Bell Inn. Further along the road is an old chapel. A few yards beyond it, in the right hand hedge, is a stile and a waymarker. Join the path and cross the watermeadows of the Avon, keeping parallel with the river some distance over to the left. Note the causeway bridge here. Lacock Abbey lies beyond the river, its splendid façade gracing this green and fertile landscape. Founded in 1232 for Augustinian nuns, it was converted to a house in the 16th century. Later it passed by marriage to the Talbot family. William Henry Fox Talbot was one of the early pioneers of photography. The National Trust owns the Abbey and the Fox Talbot Museum of Photography. Both are open to the public and well worth a visit.

Veer to the right along this stretch and make for a footbridge and stile. Go forward along the field edge to the next boundary. Cross a little stream into the next field and swing slightly right with views up towards Bowden Park and the wooded countryside encountered during the middle stages of the walk. Cross another stile and then follow the Avon riverbank, at one point crossing a stile, all the way to the road bridge. The fast-flowing Avon is quite deep along this stretch, and its banks unusually high. At the bridge bear left over the river towards some cottages. Turn left and then on the right bend go forward to join a path between several fields. On reaching some cottages by a wooden gate, bear left and go down the lane which runs through a lengthy ford further down. Take the causeway above it. Turn right into Church Street and then left by the Carpenter's Arms. At the next junction turn right and follow the road round to the George where the walk began.

⑧ Rowde
The George and Dragon

Set high above the road in the centre of Rowde, the George and Dragon has been a pub since the 1500s. Beneath the old building there are cellars where beer was once brewed, and it is said there is a tunnel or underground passage leading from the inn to the nearby church. This is highly probable as Rowde is deep in 'moonraker' country where smuggling was a regular activity. Picture if you can men at dead of night carrying barrels of illicit brandy down beneath the inn, using the secret passage to the church so they wouldn't be seen. It may seem no more than a romantic notion now, but there could just be a grain of truth in the story. The interior is charming. Note on the wall an inventory and valuation of furniture, fixtures and stock-in-trade from Mr Charles Crouch to Mr Frank Slatter in December, 1906.

Food is the priority here with fish being a speciality. The menu includes pea and ham soup, crab soufflé, crispy duck leg salad with Chinese plum sauce, pan-fried calves liver, salmon fishcakes, baked eggs and mushroom with ham, tarragon and cream, and rack of lamb. There are also fresh vegetables and green salad and a wide range of puddings. It is essential to book for food. The choice is imaginative and varied and will certainly appeal to even the more discerning gourmet. A traditional roast is available at Sunday lunchtimes. There is no food on Sunday evening or at all on Monday and the pub is closed Monday lunchtime. Real ales include Wadworth 6X and IPA. Telephone: Devizes (0380) 723053.

How to get there: Rowde is to the north west of Devizes. From Chippenham, Calne or Devizes follow the A342. The inn is on a sharp bend in the village centre.

Parking: There is a small car park at the George and Dragon. The village offers a few limited spaces and there is a car park at Caen Hill locks to the south of Rowde, with access off the B3101.

Length of the walk: 4 miles. Map: OS Landranger 173 Swindon and Devizes (GR 977626).

For those who appreciate the unique beauty of our inland waterways, this walk is a must. Beginning in the village of Rowde, the route takes the walker on a tour of the famous Caen Hill flight of locks, one of the great wonders of the canal era. Completed by John Rennie in 1810, in order to carry the Kennet and Avon Canal to a height of 237 ft, the flight consists of 29 locks in all, extending over 2 miles. The Caen Hill sequence of locks, 16 of them climbing up the hillside, has been described as the 'giant's vertebrae'. By the early 1950s the canal had fallen into decay, superseded by the road and rail network. However, canal enthusiasts, anxious to restore the Kennet and Avon to life once more, at last saw the fruits of their labours when Her Majesty the Queen reopened the canal in 1990. One of the locks on the Caen Hill flight has been named after her.

You can extend the walk by following the towpath into Devizes, where there is much to see, including Devizes Wharf, the Kennet and Avon Canal Trust headquarters and the Wadworth Brewery.

The Walk
From the front of the pub veer left into Cock Road. Pass the Tower View housing development and when you reach a junction, with The Common straight on, bear left along Sands Lane. Note the sign for the Kennet and Avon Canal. Pass a turning, Tower View, on the left. The name is pretty obvious as the dignified outline of Rowde church is clearly seen at the far end of the road, rising majestically towards the sky.

When the road swings left towards some modern houses, proceed ahead along a roughish track cutting across the fields. Bear right further on, as indicated by the yellow waymarker. Continue between fields and hedgerows. In a few minutes the track beomes more grassy, then it narrows and the hedgerows thicken. Watch out along here for

37

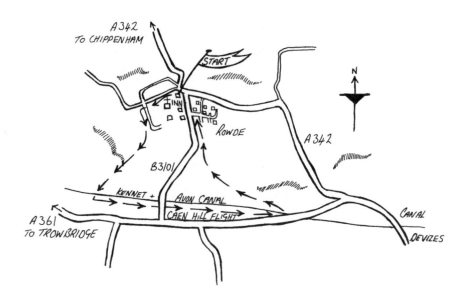

mud, particularly after heavy rain. Follow the path as it twists and turns between the trees and hedges. Eventually you come to a stile. Cross it and turn immediately right, following the field boundary. A cottage can be seen on the far side of the field. Aim for the right hand corner of the field. Cross a double stile, with a footbridge in between, and join the bank of the Kennet and Avon.

Bear left and then right, using the footbridge to cross the canal at the lock. Drop down the grassy bank to a clear track and turn left, following it alongside the canal. Pass a series of locks, part of the flight, on the approach to the road bridge. At the bridge it is worth deviating from the walk in order to admire the impressive view of the Caen Hill flight, rising to the east.

Resume the walk by passing through the tunnel and continuing along the towpath. Note the seat in memory of John Payne, who spent many happy hours fishing and walking here. Follow the towpath as it begins the gradual ascent of Caen Hill. The spectacular flight of locks grows ever nearer. A number of the locks have been named after individuals who have made various outstanding contributions to the restoration of the Kennet and Avon. Each lock has a side pound or small reservoir which ensures a constant supply of water. In the early days the canal was so busy that gas lighting was installed in order that boats could negotiate the locks day and night. Passage cost an extra shilling (5p) after dark! A world record for ascending all 29 locks was achieved in 1991 when the crew of a narrowboat came through in

38

2 hours, 6 minutes and 51 seconds. Further up, the walk reaches the Queen Elizabeth II lock, a plaque marking the spot where the Queen reopened the canal. Proceed beyond several more locks until you reach the main road at the point where it crosses the canal. Go through the tunnel under the road bridge. If you wish to visit Devizes, continue along the towpath into the town and then return to this point.

Climb the flight of steps to the bridge, cross the road and join a waymarked track leading to the British Waterways maintenance depot and manager's office. Follow the track for some distance and eventually you reach the main entrance to the depot. Pass to the right of it and go through the gate and along the track. Pass through a gate towards a farmyard and after several steps veer left to join a waymarked path (dogs should be kept on a lead). The sheltered path bypasses the farm buildings and emerges after a few yards to join a concrete track. Follow this as it runs down beside the fields. Over to the right are pleasant views over farmland, trees and hedgerows. Keep on the track as it curves to the right. At this point there is a signposted path leading to the Kennet and Avon Canal. Pass a collection of farm buildings. Continue along the track to the road. Bear right here and follow the B3101 towards Rowde. Soon the road bends left. A little further on you pass an impressive private house set in extensive grounds. Pass Rowde Court Road and proceed to the main junction in the centre of the village. Turn left by the Cross Keys and walk along the road to the George and Dragon.

⑨ Beckhampton
The Waggon and Horses

Most people who have driven along the A4 between Marlborough, Devizes or Calne easily recall this fine old 16th century thatched and stone hostelry. Serving as a local landmark, and renowned as a pub of historic distinction, the Waggon and Horses was originally a coaching inn. Built of sarsen stones from nearby Avebury, it is a charming old pub full of atmosphere and character. Open fires, mullioned windows, interconnecting rooms, wooden panelled doors, horse brasses and exposed beams greet the eye on arrival. Charles Dickens wrote about the Waggon and Horses in Chapter XIV of *Pickwick Papers*. Though not mentioning it by name, he described the pub as 'a roadside inn about half a quarter of a mile from the end of the Downs'.

The Waggon and Horses is a Wadworth pub and among the real ales are Old Timer and 6X. There is also draught cider. Children are welcome in the beer garden with play area, and the family room. There is no restaurant but good, homecooked bar meals are available every day, the choice of food being both varied and extensive. The lunchtime menu includes coachman's (roast beef and stilton) and blacksmith's (cheddar and chicken) as variations on ploughman's lunches. Vegetarian dishes include mushroom and leek flan and spinach and blue cheese crumble. There are Waggon and Horses salads, fish dishes, including smoked trout and breaded king prawns, homemade pies and chicken dishes as well as grills. Speciality sandwiches with intriguing names like Silbury Special (cheddar, onion and pineapple toasted on brown bread served with pickle), Haywain (toasted steak sandwich with a few French fries) and Horses' Bite (chicken, lettuce, bacon, tomato and mayonnaise toasted club sandwich) are featured. There are sweets and extras, plus a children's menu.

Telephone: Avebury (06723) 418.

How to get there: Beckhampton lies at the junction of the A4, the A4361 and the A361, about 7 miles west of Marlborough.

Parking: There is a car park at the rear of the inn, and some spaces at the front. You may find room in Beckhampton itself, or you could park at Avebury, beginning the circuit there.

Length of the walk: 4½ miles. Map: OS Landranger 173 Swindon and Devizes (GR 088688).

A strong sense of heritage pervades this walk, which crosses some of the loneliest and most spectacular countryside in Wiltshire. The landscape here is littered with ancient monuments to the past. Avebury, towards the end of the walk, is famous throughout the world as one of Britain's most important Bronze Age sites. It is understood to have had a religious significance, though nobody knows its true origin. The standing stones make up one of the largest remaining henge monuments, even older than Stonehenge. It is an extraordinary mystical place and the only way to really appreciate it is to go there perhaps avoiding summer weekends and bank holidays when it attracts large crowds. Avebury Manor is worth a look. It is a splendid Elizabethan manor house with mullioned windows and carved stone doorways. In the care of the National Trust, the house is open to the public.

The Walk
From the car park negotiate the double gates in the corner, go forward to the far boundary of the paddock and out to the road. Alternatively, you can follow the pavement to the roundabout near the inn, then bear right along the edge of the A4361 Swindon road for a few yards until you meet up with the path. Cross the road to the metalled lane opposite, following it towards the distant downland ridge. At the junction bear left. At the next junction, after a short distance, turn right and follow the track. On the right are the Long Stones – the first ancient relics to be found on this walk. There are good views over towards Avebury and the downs beyond. Go down to some farm

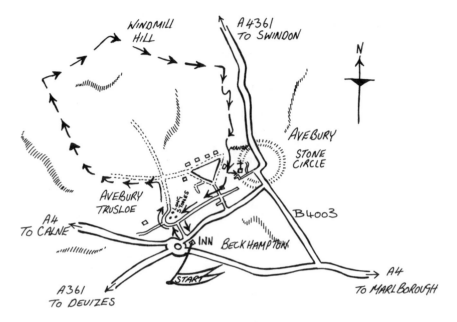

buildings and swing left at the major junction of tracks, between large open fields. Just before the track curves to the right, as you approach some farm buildings, turn right to join a rough rutted track.

When the track peters out, continue along the field edge. Note the swirling stream a few yards away from you on the right. In the field corner cross a double stile and bear right. Follow the boundary and in the corner cross another stile to a track and turn right. Follow the track through the trees. For a few moments the track hugs the edge of a field before becoming enclosed once more by trees and hedgerows. There are good views along this stretch of fields and open downland. In the distance you can just make out the slender Lansdowne obelisk rising above Cherhill Down. This was built by the 3rd Marquess in 1845 to commemorate his ancestor, Sir William Petty, a noted 17th century economist.

Look out for a track running in from the right and continue as they merge. On the right here rises Windmill Hill, in the care of the National Trust. The rounded hill has the remains of three concentric lines of earthwork dating back to about 3250 BC. Later it became a cause-wayed camp where animals were brought for slaughter. Pass a byway and just beyond it is a stile on the right, which you should cross. Beside it is a National Trust sign. Go straight up the hill and at the top there are magnificent 360° views over the entire region. Much of the route can be identified from here. One unmistakable landmark is Silbury Hill, the largest ancient man-made mound in Europe and dating from 2800 BC.

From the summit maintain the same direction over the grassy high ground as far as a stile beside a 'National Trust – sheep grazing' sign. Cross the stile and then proceed ahead along the field edge. In the corner pass through a gate and continue. On reaching the next gate, turn right and follow the field boundary. In the far corner bear left into the next field and then almost immediately right, crossing two stiles. Go obliquely right in this field, aiming for the stile in the far corner. At the next stile go forward towards the houses of Avebury. On the far side of the field, where it tapers into a corner, cross a little bridge over a stream and then bear left to another stile giving access to a raised tarmac path bordered by railings. Turn left along the path.

To look round Avebury village, follow the path until it brings you into the high street. There is much to see here and a visit to Avebury can absorb you for an hour or more.

Resuming the walk, follow the raised path almost as far as the point where you joined it, then veer left at a fork. Follow the path into a field, proceed to the next boundary and cross a stile. At the next stile join a track and follow it as it runs alongside cottages and farm buildings. On reaching the road, bear left and then right. This is South Street. Carry on along the lane and out of the village. At the junction near the Long Stones turn left and retrace your steps to the Waggon and Horses.

Lockeridge
Who'd a Thought It

The question most first time visitors to this popular pub ask is: what is the origin of its name? The answer is inside, in a written account of the pub's history. It occurred to me not to reveal the details in print but I have to admit the story is too good to leave out! The inn was established early this century by Edmund Rebbeck in what used to be the village shop. At the time, there was another pub in the village, the Mason's Arms. The landlord told Rebbeck he'd never get the licence and to forget the whole ridiculous idea. Rebbeck refused and eventually he was granted the necessary licence. When the inn opened, he exacted his revenge by calling the hostelry the 'Who'd a Thought It'.

The inn is very much a family pub, with essentially a local clientele, and specialises in homecooked food. Curry is a noted speciality. There is also soup of the day, steak and kidney pie, cottage pie, their own ham with egg and chips, fish and salad. There is a range of daily specials from the board and a children's menu. The real ales include Wadworth 6X, Old Timer, IPA, plus a guest beer, with Dry Blackthorn

Cider and various keg beers. The pub's interior comprises lounge and public bars and a dining area. Children are welcome. Dogs can come in but must be kept under control. There is a large garden and a children's play area.

Telephone: Marlborough (0672) 86255.

How to get there: The village of Lockeridge is west of Marlborough, less than a mile to the south of the A4. It is well signposted. The inn is on the right as you enter the village.

Parking: There is room to park at the inn. There is also space to park a car within the vicinity of Lockeridge Dene at the southern end of the village.

Length of the walk: 4½ miles. Map: OS Landranger 173 Swindon and Devizes (GR 147678).

Virtually all of this delightful secluded walk is under cover of trees (be prepared for mud on the forest tracks after rain). It is an ideal ramble on a bright autumn or spring morning, or perhaps a fine summer's day when the cooling canopy of branches provides a welcome respite from the heat of the sun. West Woods comprise about 600 acres of mainly beech woodland. Some of the paths on this circuit are public rights of way, while others fall within the jurisdiction of the Forestry Commission and are therefore open to the public at their discretion. However, it is extremely unlikely that access to any of the routes will be restricted. Part of the walk follows the course of the Wansdyke, a notable ditch and bank perhaps constructed as some kind of defence against possible Saxon attack.

The Walk

From the car park at the Who'd a Thought It, turn right and walk along the main street of the village passing rows of houses and cottages. Disregard a right turning to West Overton and after a few yards bear left onto a lane which, according to the sign, is 'unsuitable for heavy goods vehicles'. Follow the lane between wooded banks and at the junction go across and join a 'No Through Road'. Further up the lane it is worth glancing back for an impressive view over rolling semi-wooded country. When the track bends sharp right, continue ahead following the woodland ride as it curves left through some wooden gates. You are now entering West Woods, renowned throughout the area for their wild daffodils and hazy carpet of bluebells in spring.

The track eventually veers right and at this point bear left along a track. Pass tracks on the left and right and then take a path on the right running steeply up the hillside. Follow the path between the trees, pass over a crosstrack and continue along the main path through the

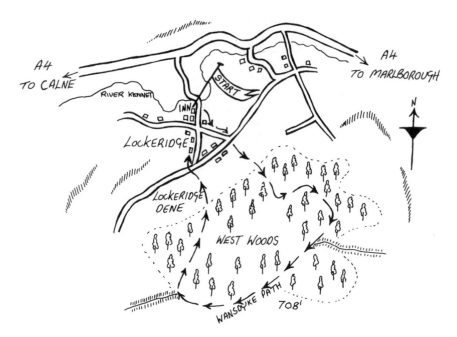

woodland. Soon there are glimpses of rolling, partly-wooded countryside up ahead. Keep to the track as it curves slightly right, keeping just inside the cover of the trees.

Further down you reach a junction with a clear track. Turn right here and then after a few yards bear sharp left onto another track. After about 50 yards swing right, onto a faint path cutting through the trees. In autumn and winter the line of the path is often concealed beneath a carpet of leaves. After a few moments you reach the Wansdyke Path. Turn right and follow it parallel with the linear earthwork. Now and again, blue and yellow symbols are visible on the tree trunks. The Wansdyke Path is 14 miles long and runs from Marlborough to Morgans Hill near Calne. The Wansdyke itself consists of a single bank and ditch. It was probably constructed by the Britons as a line of defence against the Saxons. The Britons lived south of the line, the Saxons to the north of it. Other sections of it can still be traced between Marlborough and Bristol. Looking at what remains of the Wansdyke today – a low, crumbling, grassy bank in the shade of the trees – it is hard to believe that it could ever have served a useful purpose. The density of the surrounding woodland and the close proximity of the trees seem to add an almost comical touch of irony to the role of this once vital frontier.

Pass a crosstrack and continue with the Wansdyke on your left. On

46

reaching a wide track with a yellow waymarker pointing left, cross the line of the Wansdyke and bear immediately right, onto another waymarked path. Disregard any turnings and eventually you come to a row of wooden posts providing access to a track running along the woodland edge. Pass between the posts and proceed ahead along the track with the Wansdyke on your right and open fields over to your left beyond the hedgerow. Follow the track downhill, along the extreme edge of the woodland. At the bottom of the hill, at the junction of tracks, bear sharp right avoiding the left hand track and the one going up the hill. On the right now is an area of thickish scrub and trees and on the left is dense woodland. After a few minutes the tracks fork on the edge of some pleasant undiscovered open ground ringed by trees. This is Hursley Bottom. Bear left here and follow the track up the hill into thicker woodland. You are now back in the heart of West Woods.

Further up the track, in the trees, pass over a crosstrack and proceed ahead. After a few yards cross the route of another track and continue. Follow a wide woodland ride and eventually you come up to a gate leading into a field. Keep to the right edge of the field with good views ahead. In the bottom right corner go through a gate and join an enclosed path. Descend to the road at Lockeridge Dene. The field alongside the road is strewn with sarsen stones, a common sight in Wiltshire. Several nearby cottages are built of the distinctive grey stone. Turn right and return to the car park at the Who'd a Thought It.

⑪ Ogbourne St George
The Old Crown

The Old Crown is a warm, friendly inn that is popular with local walkers and hikers undertaking the nearby Ridgeway. It is an 18th century freehouse with a floodlit well. Between Easter and October the inn is open all day for food or drink, which will come as welcome news to many Ridgeway trampers!

The single bar is small with part brick and part stone walls and the adjoining restaurant has the well, making it something of a feature. Wadworth 6X is available on handpump as well as several monthly guest ales. Lager drinkers will find Fosters and Carlsberg on offer. If a bar meal is your preference, there is a range of simple homemade food including chicken and mushroom, and steak and kidney pies. Sandwiches are available daily. The restaurant menu (booking advisable) includes duck in honey and orange sauce, and chicken stuffed with stilton. There is a traditional roast on Sunday. The Old Crown also provides bed and breakfast. Outside is a small garden with a children's play area. Dogs are welcome.

Telephone: Marlborough (0672) 84445.

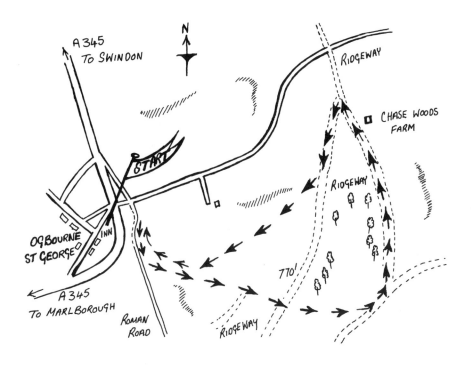

How to get there: Ogbourne St George is between Marlborough and Swindon, just off the A345. The Old Crown is in the village centre.

Parking: There is usually room to park at The Old Crown. If not, there may be some spaces in the main street or along the road almost opposite the inn.

Length of the walk: 4½ miles. Map: OS Landranger 174 Newbury and Wantage (GR 203742).

This spectacular walk is in typical Wiltshire downland country, much of it far removed from signs of civilisation, roads, houses and the usual reminders of modern life. Almost immediately, it climbs high above the village of Ogbourne St George, at length disappearing into an enclosed land of bare hills and woods. The final stage of the walk is along the Ridgeway, a route of great antiquity. Now a long distance footpath, it was originally a major east-west route in prehistoric Britain. From this high ground there are magnificent views across to Barbury Castle. This is an Iron Age hillfort of about 12 acres. The site is named after Bera, a tribal chief. Wiltshire County Council has created a popular country park here.

49

The Walk

Turn right, out of the car park, and pass beneath the A345 flyover. Bear right signposted 'Bytham Farm'. Walk along the lane – part of a Roman road – and the main road and an old disused railway line are just a few yards away on the right. Glancing over to the westerly horizon, you will spot the outline of Barbury Castle. Go past a cottage and on reaching a sign 'Auto Plant Services', bear left and proceed up the track. Pass the light industrial plant on the right. Beyond it carry on up the track between hedgerows. Further up, it is worth pausing to look back for a spectacular view over to Barbury Castle, with Ogbourne St George in the foreground.

At the top of the hill merge with the Ridgeway and follow it for a short distance until you reach a junction of tracks. Ignore left and right turnings and keep ahead. Pass some small farm buildings amongst the trees. This stretch of the walk provides distant glimpses of the downland country where it reaches down to the Kennet valley. The track makes a gradual descent. Pass a turning on the left down to a farm and continue between lines of trees. Soon you merge with another track. Ignore tracks right and left and after several minutes you reach a fork. Take the left hand track, ignoring the turning to Stock Lane. Keep on the track as it cuts between fields and bursts of woodland. Eventually, you come up to some barns, various old farm buildings and cottages. Go over a cattle grid and pass the entrance to a solitary house on the edge of the trees over to the right. Pass over another grid and continue beyond several more houses.

Take the sharp left hand track, rejoining the Ridgeway, and follow it between trees and hedgerows. There are good downland views to the right. From here you can spot traffic on the main A345. The Ridgeway tends to be wide in places, as when the original line became weathered or difficult to negotiate, the traveller moved to one side and so made the track wider. After several minutes or so, look for a path on the right. It runs down the slope, cutting between fences and hedgerows. Take the path and follow it, with excellent views of Ogbourne St George, and Barbury Castle rising above it. Keep on the path, with clear uninterrupted views. Further down, the path joins the track you came up at the start of the walk. Follow it down the hill, turn right at the junction and, at the road junction, bear left to the pub car park.

⑫ Fox Hill
The Shepherd's Rest

This quaint old Flowers inn has the distinction of being the only pub directly on the route of the Ridgeway. Originally, it was favoured by drovers and shepherds who used the route to transport their cattle and sheep. The Ridgeway crosses the Ermine Way at this point – the old Roman road running from Silchester to Cirencester and Gloucester. But it is the inn's position on one of Britain's most popular national trails that has helped to establish the Shepherd's Rest as a local landmark and a noted hostelry with a warm, friendly atmosphere. Its lounge bar in particular has not been modernised and the traditional atmosphere adds to its appeal. The bar has a log fire in winter, a low beamed ceiling and prints with a horse racing theme, which is appropriate for a pub whose clientele is partly represented by local members of the racing fraternity. Lambourn is nearby and there are many racing stables within a stone's throw of the inn.

Food is available seven days a week, both sessions. The menu is extensive – so much so that you almost feel spoilt for choice. Soup of the day and shepherd's mushrooms are among the starters. There are fish dishes, including scampi and halibut parmesan, the 'Shepherd's Monster Mixed Grill' for the hearty appetite, Wiltshire gammon and chicken Mexico. There is a good choice of lighter meals and snacks too, including hot savouries and open sandwiches, salads, ploughman's and jacket potatoes. Vegetarians are not excluded either, mushroom stroganoff and ratatouille topped with melted cheese being among the dishes available. On Sundays there is a traditional roast. There is no need to book for meals in the bar but it would be advisable to do so if you would like to eat in the restaurant, particularly at the weekend. Real ales include Flowers IPA and Original and Wadworth 6X. There is also a guest beer as well as Bulmers Draught Cider and Heineken Lager. Children are welcome as long as they are having a meal and there is a play area for them in the garden. The inn does not provide accommodation but camping is permitted in the garden, with toilet and shower facilities available.

Telephone: Swindon (0793) 790266.

How to get there: Fox Hill is just outside Swindon, near the village of Wanborough. From Marlborough follow the A345 and bear right for Wanborough and Fox Hill. From Hungerford and Swindon take the B4192. The inn is at the crossroads near Wanborough. Junction 15 of the M4 is close by.

Parking: There is room to park at the front and side of the inn. Fox Hill is a hamlet in rather remote country, therefore other opportunities for parking are limited.

Length of the walk: 4½ miles. Map: OS Landranger 174 Newbury and Wantage (GR 231814).

The glorious wide open spaces of Wiltshire, the sense of history and freedom, and the timeless appeal of that prehistoric route known as the Ridgeway are all perfectly reflected in this walk across the North Wessex Downs. The downs rise to 800 ft as you join the Ridgeway, now one of the Countryside Commission's national trails, stretching for 85 miles between Avebury and Ivinghoe Beacon. Our route covers only about a mile of it but the feeling of peace and tranquillity on these downs is second to none.

The return leg is via two pretty villages, Bishopstone and Hinton Parva, with some road walking along quiet lanes. Strings of horses may be seen from time to time on the route.

The Walk
From the front of the inn bear left to the crossroads, then left again heading towards Hinton Parva and Bishopstone. When the road curves left after about 150 yards, leave it and join the unmetalled Ridgeway, signposted 'Wayland's Smithy, Uffington Castle and

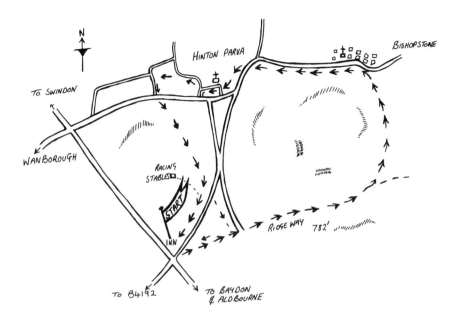

Streatley'. The path begins a gradual ascent to climb up between Charlbury Hill and Fox Hill with the outline of a transmitter on the hilltop on the right. Pass the route of a bridleway and press on over this breezy ground. On the left are grand views over north Wiltshire towards the Vale of the White Horse. Ignore a turning on the left and continue.

Further on, there are glorious views stretching to the horizon. On a good day the cooling towers of Didcot power station are visible. The Ridgeway begins to descend between hedgerows. Keep on the main path and when it levels out, bear left to join a waymarked bridleway. Aim for a fold in the downs ahead and follow the bridleway. The track can be wet and muddy after rain, but there are parallel paths which may be drier. Go through a gate and follow the field edge to the corner. Bear right and join a track, following it through a kissing gate. A little later the track swings left between hedgerows. Eventually, you reach the road.

Turn left and walk through the village of Bishopstone. The church may be glimpsed on the right. Head out of the village and follow the road between fields. At the junction veer left, signposted 'Wanborough'. After a short distance look for a stile and some railings in the bank on the right. Cross into the field and go forward to the far boundary. Pass through a kissing gate and proceed ahead to the next boundary. Here you negotiate a dilapidated old kissing gate beside a

53

wrought iron gate. Go forward along a somewhat overgrown path. Note the churchyard on your right. At the road, in the centre of the pretty village of Hinton Parva, turn right and after a few yards bear right again opposite some thatched cottages. Follow the road round the left bend and on the next bend, beside the Mission Hall, leave the road and follow the footpath, signposted 'The Grove', down to a kissing gate. Go along a straight path beyond, cutting between fields. At the road turn left and in a couple of minutes or so you reach another junction. Cross over at this point and follow the waymarked bridleway running alongside the village hall. Further on, it narrows to a path and climbs gradually high above the fields and downland. Looking back, there are very good views to the north, with the houses of Hinton Parva in the foreground.

Pass through a gate and continue, crossing the all-weather training gallops. The buildings of Stan Mellor's racing stables come into view on the right. The yard is named Pollardstown, after a noted racehorse of recent times. On reaching the road you have a choice. To avoid any more road walking, continue over the road and along the next stretch of bridleway until you reach the Ridgeway. Turn right and follow it back to the inn. Alternatively, return to the Shepherd's Rest by bearing right and following the road all the way. It is essentially a quiet lane, so there should be no problems about heavy traffic.

⑬ Ramsbury
The Bell

The Bell is a 300 year old former coaching inn, which, I am told, does not have a ghost! The freehouse stands at the very heart of Ramsbury, looking out over the square and the main street beyond. Inside, the pub comprises many attractive features. In the modernised bar, divided by a large chimney breast, there are original beams, some exposed brick and stone work and a roaring log fire, cosy and welcoming on a winter's day. The walls are adorned with paintings and sketches including many wildlife and hunting scenes. Look for the Victorian stained glass panel in the front window.

As far as real ales go, several old favourites are available, including Wadworth 6X and IPA ·Henry's Original. There is also a guest beer. Carlsberg and Lowenbrau are among the choice of lagers. The Bell has a good varied menu. Starters or snacks include smoked mackerel pâté and toast, Thai butterfly prawns, soup of the day and deep fried brie and cranberry sauce. Cumberland sausage ring and Wiltshire grill are among the grills and steaks. For those who like something spicy there is the ever popular Jambalaya – pieces of chicken and gammon, pan fried with tarragon and garlic and mixed with savoury rice. Venison casserole is another of the noted specialities. There are also fish and

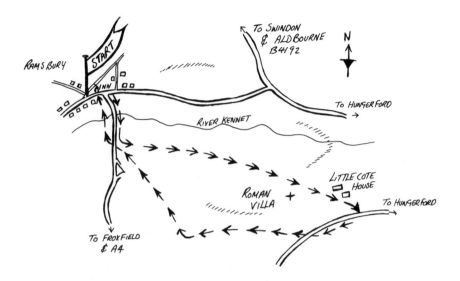

vegetarian dishes, plus a selection of sandwiches and jacket potatoes, homemade puddings and sweets. Food is not available on Sunday evenings, except between May and September. There is a beer garden. This is a popular pub and it is advisable to book for meals, especially for larger parties.

Telephone: Marlborough (0672) 20230.

How to get there: Ramsbury is east of Marlborough. From the town you can cut across country through Mildenhall and Axford. From Swindon or Hungerford follow the B4192 and turn off at the sign. The Bell is in the village square.

Parking: There is a car park at the rear of The Bell and there is usually room to park elsewhere in the vicinity of the inn.

Length of the walk: 5 miles. Map: OS Landranger 174 Newbury and Wantage (GR 276716).

Between AD 908 and 1058 Ramsbury was a bishopric. Today, it is a large village popular with locals and city commuters. One of its most famous features was the huge hollow elm in the village square. It had to be cut down in the 1980s and replaced by an oak tree, the planting of which was sponsored by what was the Ramsbury Building Society.

The walk follows the bank of the river Kennet, a popular haunt of wildlife. In springtime black swans may be seen on the river, and Canada and Brent geese also nest here. The route crosses the grounds of Littlecote Park, passing right alongside the magnificent 15th century brick-built mansion. The house is open to the public and includes many fine treasures. The Great Hall and the Long Gallery are well worth ·a look.

The Walk

Leave the car park by turning left. This is Scholards Lane. After a few moments bear right (signposted 'Froxfield'). On the right here is The Old Mill, an attractive old house on the Kennet. On reaching a signposted path to Littlecote House (2 miles), turn left and follow the track alongside a house. Pass the buildings and ignore a bridleway branching off half right. Keep ahead on the main track as it runs parallel to the meandering Kennet. The houses of Ramsbury are still visible over the tops of the hedgerows. Continue through a pleasant semi-wooded landscape, with the river never far away.

A little later you reach a house. Proceed beyond it, noting the river running along the bottom of the garden. Follow the bridleway as it cuts along the edge of a field. There is a belt of woodland providing glimpses of the river down below among the trees. On the right here is the site of a Roman villa. The Roman mosaic was originally unearthed early in the 18th century. However, it was reburied by the then owner in a bid to preserve it. Years later, in the 1970s, it was uncovered and has been carefully and painstakingly restored. It is thought to date back to around AD 360.

Eventually, the parkland of Littlecote comes into view. Soon the house itself can be seen. Follow a clear drive between rows of young trees towards it. During the spring, summer and early autumn, Littlecote House is open to the public. The grounds are often crowded with visitors, many of whom come to enjoy the popular jousting arena, which you can see over to the right.

Proceed along the drive as it runs beside the house. Follow it along an avenue of lime trees as far as the brick and flint lodge at the main gate. Turn right and go up the road through the trees. There are good views of the Kennet valley over to the right. When the road bends sharp left, continue ahead to join a track signposted 'Ramsbury 2½ miles'. There is a gate here between brick pillars. You are now re-entering the grounds of Littlecote. Follow the drive through the estate, wooded on this stretch. At the right hand bend go straight on, noting the splendid view of Littlecote House, with the hills of north east Wiltshire rising behind it. There are glimpses of the outward leg of this walk at this stage.

Drop down the steep decline to another right hand turning and continue past the 'Private, No Through Road' sign. There is a yellow waymarker arrow beneath it – so don't worry! The track leaves the

57

parkland of Littlecote behind it now and cuts between fields and bursts of light woodland. At the end of a line of old beeches, the track veers a little to the right to reach a junction. Bear right and follow a track with a concrete surface, passing a track running in from the left. Go round to the right and up the hill, with light woodland on the right.

When the track bends right and cuts deeper into the trees, go straight on along a muddy bridleway. Further down, the path forks and in front of you are good views of Ramsbury and the Kennet valley. Take either path, as they join up further down the bank. Carry on down the bridleway between the hedgerows, skirt the edge of a large field and at the junction turn left along the track to the road. You will probably recognise this part of the route from the initial stages of the walk. At the road bear right and retrace your steps to Ramsbury.

⒕ Little Bedwyn
The Harrow

The Harrow is a fully restored Victorian pub located on the edge of Little Bedwyn, a delightful village situated on a picturesque stretch of the Kennet and Avon Canal. It has an interesting background. For many years it was a traditional local, with the village post office operated from the back, and its closure in 1990 was received with the utmost dismay. It stayed firmly shut until some of its most loyal customers, frustrated at having to travel to neighbouring villages for a drink, formed a consortium and bought the pub themselves. The inn was then given a completely new lease of life and officially re-opened in 1991 by local television personality Johnny Morris, a keen supporter of The Harrow and a regular drinker there over the years.

These days, the inn, which also provides accommodation, has a front room and two inner rooms whose stylish decor give The Harrow a chic upmarket feel. There is a selection of real ales including one of the Hook Norton brews, as well as several guest beers. Light meals are

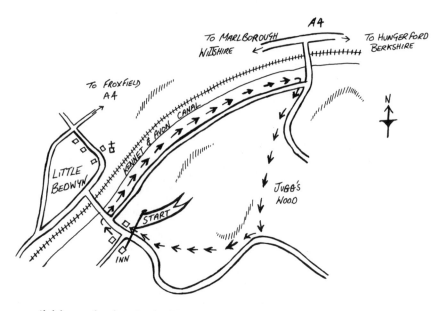

available at the bar including potato and herb soup, sautéd kidneys and marinated vegetables, sirloin steak sandwich and chicken and watercress filo pie. Among other specialities, the restaurant menu offers fillet steak stuffed with blue cheese and baked skate with a herb crust. There are homemade puddings and a cheeseboard. The choice of freshly prepared dishes is varied and the food at The Harrow has a growing reputation for making use of local ingredients. The Harrow, which has a beer garden, is closed Monday lunchtimes and no food is available on Sunday and Monday evenings. It is advisable to book a table in the restaurant, which is a no smoking area. Dogs, families and walkers are made very welcome.

Telephone: Marlborough (0672) 870871.

How to get there: Little Bedwyn lies just to the south of the A4 on the Wiltshire/Berkshire boundary. Leave the A4 at Froxfield and on reaching Little Bedwyn cross the canal and the railway and follow the road signposted Bagshot for a short distance. The inn is on the right.

Parking: The Harrow does not have a car park, but, depending on custom, there is room to park at the front of the inn or in the road at the side of it.

Length of the walk: 3½ miles. Map: OS Landranger 174 Newbury and Wantage (GR 293657).

60

Little Bedwyn is smaller than its near neighbour, Great Bedwyn, and is an equally charming village. The Kennet and Avon Canal and the Paddington – West Country main line railway divide it into two distinct halves. The walk follows the canal towpath until it reaches the Berkshire border at Froxfield. The return leg to Little Bedwyn is a pleasant stroll along green tracks and quiet country paths.

The Walk

From The Harrow, walk down the street to the junction. Go straight across and down the 'No through road'. On reaching the Kennet and Avon Canal by Little Bedwyn lock, you have a choice. To visit the rest of the village and its historic church, cross the footbridge over the water and the railway line; then retrace your steps to this point. However, if this is not part of your itinerary, you will want to start the walk proper. To do this, follow the canal towpath heading in an easterly direction towards Froxfield. Along this stretch there are good views of Little Bedwyn church and the surrounding buildings.

Pass some canalside cottages to reach a bridge. Continue along the towpath for some distance. At length it runs alongside the road. In a moment or two, you reach Oakhill Down lock. The stretch of canal between Hungerford west and Little Bedwyn was re-opened to navigation in 1977; a commemorative plaque recalls the occasion.

Proceed alongside the canal as road and waterway part company. Pass Froxfield Bottom Lock and then continue a little further to the

road bridge over the Kennet and Avon. The bridge forms the county boundary between Wiltshire and Berkshire. Leave the canal and go up the bank to join the road. Turn right and follow the road. On the right at this point is an attractive house with a lake often inhabited by ducks and swans.

Continue on the road and at the right hand bend go straight on along the road signposted North Standen. Follow the lane through some delightful unspoilt countryside. When it bends sharp left, continue ahead along a track with woodland hard on your right. Eventually, with Jugg's Wood on the right, the track veers to the right. There is a junction of tracks at this point, with a turning on the left and a straight track in front of you running across the fields towards hedgerows and distant trees. Take this track and follow it over the open ground. Soon it narrows to a path running between trees and bushes. Shortly, you join the road on a sharp bend. Turn right and follow the single track lane for about 100 yards.

Take the waymarked path on the right and cross the field diagonally to the far boundary. There is woodland over on the left. If it is easier, follow the field perimeter in a clockwise direction. On reaching the far corner of the field, pass through the exit and go forward into the next field, using the distinctive white farm buildings down below as a directional landmark. The actual route of the walk, however, veers a little to the right at this stage, cutting diagonally across the fields until it emerges at the road via a stile. (Sometimes there are electric fences in this field, in which case head straight down the track towards the road and on reaching the double gates in front of the farm buildings turn right and follow the field edge along a grassy track as far as the stile.)

Turn right, walk down the lane and The Harrow will be found on the left after several minutes.

15 Wilton
The Swan

The Swan, situated at the heart of this quiet village, is a pre-war building thought to date back to the 1920s. Before moving to its present site, the inn was located a short distance along the road. It is a traditional, unpretentious village pub, the sort frequented by faithful regulars who can recall its history and that of the village, going back over many years. It is essentially a locals' pub, but it is also popular with passing motorists in search of the nearby pumping station and windmill. The Swan is a freehouse with an authentic, unspoilt character. There is a spacious single bar with a high ceiling, old black and white photographs and horse brasses, and a restaurant in one corner. Real ales include Wadworth 6X and the Swan's own bitter. Draught cider is available as well as Carlsberg Export, Heineken, and Murphy's Stout.

A good varied menu includes vegetable soup and sandwiches and there are many homemade dishes to sample. For something a little more substantial, there is chicken and ham pie, steak pie, liver and

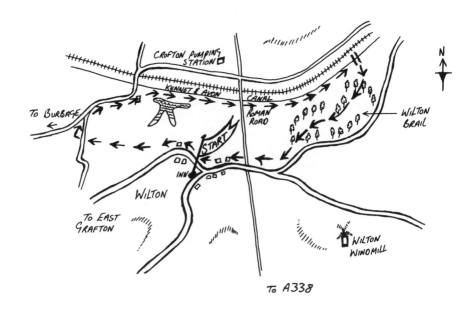

bacon grill and rump or gammon steak (with pineapple or egg). The menu changes on a regular basis and salads and lighter meals are also available during the summer. There is a garden including a playground for children. Large groups are advised to book in advance for food.

Telephone: Marlborough (0672) 870274.

How to get there: Wilton is about 7 miles south west of Hungerford, just off the A338 Andover road. From Marlborough head south to Burbage and East Grafton. Wilton is signposted.

Parking: There is room to park at The Swan. Alternatively you could park in the layby opposite the Wilton windmill. It is about ½ mile from here to the centre of Wilton, where the walk begins.

Length of the walk: 3½ miles. Map: OS Landranger 174 Newbury and Wantage (GR 267614).

Wilton is a quiet, pretty village, famous in the area for its duck pond. Nearby is the 19th century Wilton windmill, restored to working order in the 1970s by the Wiltshire Historic Buildings Trust. Open to the public at various times, it can be seen on the higher ground of this most enjoyable walk.

Our walk leaves Wilton and soon reaches the towpath of the Kennet and Avon Canal. On the right is Wilton Water, an 8 acre reservoir rising from natural springs

64

and supplying water to the canal's summit level. The restored Crofton Pumping Station, re-opened by Sir John Betjeman, pumps the water from the reservoir into the canal. Superseded by electricity in 1958, the 19th century steam engines are well worth a visit. The pumping station is open to the public at certain times. The walk returns to Wilton via a lovely pheasant wood known as Wilton Brail.

The Walk

From the inn bear left and walk along the main street of the village. Pass the duck pond and follow the road round to the left. Note the Methodist church on the left. Continue up the hill. At the top turn right by some houses to join a track (Upper Brooklands). In a while pass through a gateway and descend the field by keeping to the right boundary. In the bottom corner cross the stile into the woodland. The path drops down briefly and in wet weather the bank here can be quite slippery. Cross the footbridge and, once over the next stile, head out across the field. Over to the right can be seen the distinctive buildings of Crofton Pumping Station.

Aim for the stile ahead, a little to the left of some farm buildings. Cross it to the next stile, then emerge into the road. Turn right and continue past the farm entrance, keeping to the road as it bends left. At the junction turn right to reach the Kennet and Avon Canal. The lock here is named after Samuel William Farmer, agriculturalist and philanthropist, who lived at Little Bedwyn Manor between 1874 and 1926. As the notice says, 'Funds towards restoring this lock were donated by the Samuel William Farmer Trust in 1987'.

Turn right and follow the towpath in an easterly direction towards Great Bedwyn. The railway line is on your left, a few yards away. Pass the next lock and continue ahead. Soon the buildings of Crofton Pumping Station are clearly visible on the opposite bank. Pass Crofton flight, re-opened by the Hon Charles Morrison MP and Michael McNair-Wilson MP on 6th October 1988.

Note Wilton Water at this stage of the walk. The reservoir attracts various species of birdlife, including the tufted duck, mallard, pochard and teal.

At the next lock you have a choice. If you wish to visit the pumping station, cross the railway at the gates and follow the road down to the junction. Bear left and follow the road to the main entrance. Retrace your steps to the canal and continue along the towpath in an easterly direction. Pass another lock. Go under a brick-built bridge, and over on the left you will see a solitary house. On reaching Beechgrove Lock, bear right and go through the wooden gate. Follow the right edge of the field up to the edge of the woodland. Under the trees pass through a gap, ignoring the signposted path on the left, and continue ahead for a few yards. At the junction veer right and follow a clear waymarked path through the woods. This is Wilton Brail, a favourite haunt of pheasants.

Keep to the main path as it plunges deeper into the woodland. Occasionally, there are white arrows to be found on the tree trunks, pointing the direction ahead. After some time, when the path begins to veer to the right, begin to head over to the left towards the edge of the woods, where you will see a waymarker post and a small bridge over a pond. Follow the path out of the woods, with the ridge of the North Hampshire Downs visible in the distance. Cross a stile and follow the field boundary. In the corner cross two stiles and then join a clear path across the next field. This is high breezy ground with good views. Wilton windmill can be seen from here. Descend the slope towards Wilton. At the junction of paths bear right, down the slope to the track. Turn left to the road, swinging right to follow it back into Wilton. The Swan is on the left.

⓯ Upavon
The Antelope

First mentioned in 1609, the Antelope was rebuilt early in the 18th century. Originally, it was a coaching inn for passengers travelling between London and Bath. Upavon also had a thriving market at one time and no doubt the inn derived much business from the local trade. The antelope, from which the pub name originates, is a swift-running, deer-like animal introduced around the 11th century for the sport of kings.

The Antelope's landlord, Christos Constantinou, has introduced various Greek dishes on the daily specials board! The long bar at the front is cosy and friendly and the bow-windowed games room next door is very popular. The Antelope, which also provides accommodation, is essentially a family pub and has been the recipient of a food award and a stay award. The inn serves food seven days a week and at both sessions. Among the dishes are cheddar ploughman's, T-bone steak and sirloin steak, scampi, ocean pie, steak and kidney pie, country pie, soup of the day, sandwiches and salads. The menu also caters for children. There is also a separate restaurant

with the emphasis increasingly on bistro. Real ales include Wadworth 6X (the Antelope is a Wadworth house) and Farmer's Glory. Outside there is a beer garden with a play area for children.
Telephone: Amesbury (0980) 630206.

How to get there: The Antelope is at the heart of Upavon. The village lies at the junction of the A342 and the A345, between Marlborough and Salisbury.

Parking: There are spaces at the front and rear of the inn. Alternatively, there are some parking spaces a few yards away in front of the public conveniences.

Length of the walk: 4¼ miles. Maps: OS Landranger 173 Swindon and Devizes, 184 Salisbury and the Plain (GR 134549).

The scenery offered by this walk is surely some of the finest to be found anywhere within the boundaries of Wiltshire. There is a splendid mixture of high exposed downland providing stunning views to the Vale of Pewsey and beyond, and, during the latter stages of the walk, gentle sheltered countryside around the watermeadows at the head of the Avon valley.

Until around the beginning of the 19th century, there was a bustling market at Upavon. The meeting point of two important routes also helped to bring trade to the village, and to establish Upavon as a vital and prosperous community between the towns of Andover, Marlborough and Devizes. Not surprisingly, the old market square is still the focal point of the village. As well as the restored church with its castellated tower and octagonal Norman font, there are a number of picturesque old buildings worth closer inspection.

The Walk
From the front of the Antelope turn right and then immediately left onto the A342, signposted to Andover. Walk along the main road (don't worry – there's a pavement!) between houses and cottages. On the right hand bend go straight on to join a path running up beside Braybrooke Pottery. Follow the path between the houses until, further up, it cuts between banks of trees and undergrowth. At length, the banks and hedgerows give way to reveal superb downland views back toward the Avon valley and the village of Upavon.

Join a firm track and continue over this high breezy ground. Over to the right, in the distance, the houses of RAF Upavon can easily be glimpsed. In the foreground, the fairways of a golf course gradually become visible. Keep going over the top of the downs. The track is fainter now but still apparent. When the track forks, veer right, aiming towards the left edge of the RAF station.

68

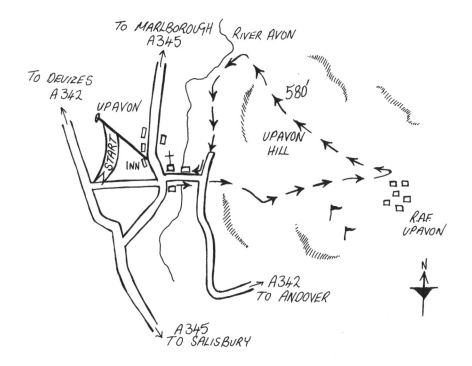

After the First World War RAF flying instructors undertook their training here, and before the start of the Second World War Upavon became a base for fighter squadrons when experimental night flying exercises were carried out. After the war transport and strike commands continued to be based here. Nowadays, however, Upavon's role in defence is a mainly administrative one.

Follow the track, with outstanding views across to a broad sweep of downland over to the left. Further on, when you reach a clear track, bear sharp left and head in a north westerly direction, the buildings of RAF Upavon behind you. Follow the track between fences, with magnificent views over the downs to the Vale of Pewsey beyond. Over to the left, beyond the Avon valley, the downs rise up towards the edge of Salisbury Plain. At this stage of the walk you are more than 500 ft above sea level. Pass a track on the right and continue.

The route begins a gradual descent, and runs alongside a belt of trees with the woodland becoming thicker further down. There is now a line of trees and bushes on your left. At the bottom of the slope, down in the valley, you reach a junction of tracks. Bear left here onto a waymarked path. The scenery on this stretch of the walk is

69

considerably softer and altogether more pastoral as the route leaves the bleak downs and explores the fields and watermeadows of the Avon valley.

Follow the track between fences, with the Avon a short distance away to the right. Stay on the track, muddy in places, as it cuts between fields and watermeadows. There is a parallel line of telegraph poles along this part of the route. Pass several old corrugated barns, and a bridleway on the left. Join a metalled lane and follow it with houses on the left and very pleasant views on the right over to Upavon church and a cluster of pretty cottages beyond the watermeadows.

At the junction turn right and retrace your steps along the A342 back into the centre of Upavon, passing on the right the Parish Reading Room, erected to commemorate the coronation of George V in 1911.

⑰ Limpley Stoke
The Hop Pole

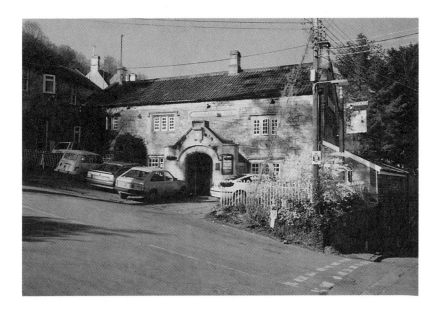

The Hop Pole, a freehouse, is a superb example of a genuine unpretentious pub. In many respects it is how ethnic country inns used to be before many of them were deprived of a sense of identity. As if that wasn't tempting enough, there is also an intriguing tale of monks and secret tunnels! The history of this inn is described in some detail inside. Deriving its name from a hop plant, it apparently dates back to the late 16th century. Before then there may have been a monks' wine lodge on this site, and part of an older building still remains, thought to date back to about 1300. Monks traded with wool at Bradford on Avon and often crossed the ford at Limpley Stoke. They may have stayed the night at the wine house, using it as a halfway house during their travels. There is understood to be a secret tunnel which runs down to the Avon from here, enabling the monks to get down to the river secretly and safely at night. The site of an old mill there may have been where they met in secret. Some kind of tunnel was discovered by drainage workmen in the 1960s, adding credence to the story.

There are two bars at the Hop Pole. One of them is called the Avon bar which is mainly for eating, the other one is known as the Valley bar and is smaller and very cosy. Both bars have dark oak panelled walls. There is also a charming room at the back for families or large parties. The food is varied and wholesome, with freshly made soup and melon sorbet cocktail among the starters. Main courses include steak and ale pie, goujon of plaice, Cumberland sausage with apple and onion in a French stick, and Porterhouse steak. Some dishes only served in the evening include salmon wrapped in pastry with a parsley sauce and baked halibut with garlic and herb butter. There is also a selection of winter specials and a range of salads. Food is not available on Sunday evenings, but there is a traditional roast at lunchtime. Real ales are Courage Best, Wadworth 6X, Bass, Marston's Pedigree and a guest beer. There is an attractive garden at the rear, where summer barbecues take place. Larger parties are asked to book for food.

Telephone: Limpley Stoke (0225) 723124.

How to get there: Limpley Stoke lies to the south east of Bath. From the city and Bradford on Avon follow the B3108. At a sharp bend by a railway bridge, join the road marked Lower Stoke. The pub is on the right at Woods Hill.

Parking: The easiest place to park is in the Hop Pole car park across the road, near the railway line. The village itself offers limited room for parking.

Length of the walk: 4½ miles. Map: OS Landranger 172 Bristol and Bath (GR 782612).

The wooded Avon valley in all its splendour is the thread running through this delightful walk. From the Hop Pole the route follows the towpath of the Kennet and Avon Canal, with the river Avon parallel across the fields, as far as John Rennie's classic 19th century masterpiece, the Dundas Aqueduct, which, with its Bath stone façade and fine Doric columns, blends perfectly into this spectacular landscape.

From the waterway the walk climbs steeply through some woods to reach the higher ground, where there are grand views across Wiltshire. Eventually, you reach the picturesque village of Winsley before descending into the valley once more. The return leg to Limpley Stoke is along a further section of canal towpath.

The Walk
From the front of the pub (or the enclosed garden at the back), bear left and walk down the lane, keeping the railway line on the right. Turn right at the main road, passing under the railway. Follow the B3108, crossing the Avon, and go on up the hill as far as the bridge over the Kennet and Avon Canal. Bear left to cross the stile, joining the towpath and heading in a northerly direction. As you progress

72

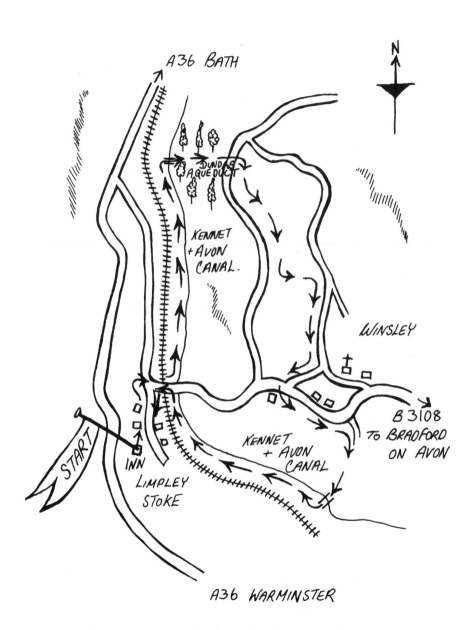

A36 BATH

N

DUNDAS AQUEDUCT

KENNET + AVON CANAL.

WINSLEY

B 3108 To BRADFORD ON AVON

START

INN

LIMPLEY STOKE

KENNET + AVON CANAL

A36 WARMINSTER

along the towpath, you will see that the opposite bank is well wooded, while to the left there are excellent views over the valley and back towards Limpley Stoke, its houses of distinctive Bath stone clinging to the steep wooded slopes. In the distance there are glimpses of a viaduct carrying traffic through the valley and on towards Bath.

Pass the remains of a disused lock and then follow the towpath as the canal bends left. Almost at once, the splendid Dundas Aqueduct comes into view, its graceful classical design adding a touch of elegance to the restored canal. At the point where the aqueduct passes over the Avon and the Bristol – Southampton railway, there is a wonderful view of the valley and its broad-leaved trees. However, the surroundings are deceptively tranquil, for apart from the aqueduct, there is the river and the railway line, and, parallel to them, a busy main road – all four lines of communication cutting a narrow passage here.

Further along the towpath is a footbridge at the junction with the charmingly-named Somersetshire Coal Canal, opened in 1801. Part of the canal was restored in 1986-88 for moorings and boat base. A notice here advises canal travellers that this is a 'Private garden – boat skippers please stop here and pick up crew before proceeding through the lock'. Bear right and pass the remains of Dundas Wharf. Charles Dundas was Chairman of the Kennet and Avon Canal Company. Note the plaque which reads 'Kennet and Avon Canal Trust unveiled this plaque in the presence of Sir Frank Price to celebrate the restoration of this aqueduct and to record its appreciation for the help and encouragement he afforded the Trust during his Chairmanship of the British Waterways Board, 1st July 1984.'

Continue along the towpath as far as the footbridge. Cross the canal at this point and turn right, ignoring the route to Claverton. The arches of the Dundas aqueduct can be seen through the trees. Walk along the towpath high above the Avon and the railway line. Looking north at this stage reveals a splendid vista along the valley floor towards wooded hills rising up in the distance. A left hand path, descending the bank via a flight of wooden steps, provides the opportunity to gaze up at the aqueduct. You need to walk a few yards over the watermeadows in order to appreciate the full splendour of the mighty structure.

Return to the top path and when the canal swings right, go straight on to join a path running up over a stile and into Conkwell Wood. Further up, go through another stile and proceed up the steep hillside. At the top, on reaching a junction, turn right by a wire fence and follow the path to the road. Continue ahead, following the road round a left bend and past Copt Oak and Little Park Manor. In the gateway here is a splendid view stretching to the distant downs on the horizon.

On the next right angled bend, go through a gap in the wall and cross the field to the boundary. Pass into the next field and follow the edge to the exit in the far right corner. Go out to a lane and bear right. At the junction, on the outskirts of Winsley, turn right, passing a left turning (Late Broads). At the triangular junction, bear left into Limpley Stoke Road. Pass the Sutcliffe School and the Methodist church. At the left hand bend in the centre of Winsley, take the right turning signposted 'Village Hall and Bowls Club'.

At the fork in front of some gates, bear right and after a few yards veer right onto a path running between stone walls. It later descends some steps and reaches a fork. Bear left here. There are good views over towards Limpley Stoke. The path plunges into the valley by a series of steps. Either side of you are houses and gardens. Cross a lane serving various residences and continue down the next flight of steps towards the Kennet and Avon Canal.

Further down you reach a stile. Cross it into the field and make for the next boundary. On reaching it, join a track and turn right, crossing a bridge to the far bank of the canal. Turn right to join the towpath. This stretch of waterway is particularly attractive, as it runs beside wooded banks and offers delightful views to the left of the Avon down below in the fields. Pass several houses and cottages, some with gardens running down to the water's edge. Later on, the houses of Limpley Stoke loom through the trees. Note the entrance to Fordside Tea Garden on the left. Once you have gone through the tunnel, leave the towpath to join the B3108. Walk down to the railway bridge and bear left back to the Hop Pole.

⑱ Wingfield
The Poplars

The Poplars has been a pub since the early 1950s. Prior to that it was an off licence and village shop. The whitewashed building is about 250 years old and was originally a farmhouse. The Poplars is a classic English pub with all the right ingredients. But there is something else that sets it apart from the rest. The inn has its own cricket ground, an innovation introduced by a previous landlord. During the cricket season the Poplars can become extremely busy when teams and supporters gather in the lounge and public bars to celebrate and commiserate. Here, there is a very strong cricketing theme, with photographs and prints of the game adorning the walls.

There is a choice of real ale. Old Timer is available in winter and Farmer's Glory in summer. There is also Wadworth 6X and IPA. The food is homecooked and includes a selection of snacks, such as toasted sandwiches, including cheese and ham, and bacon and mushroom, ploughman's lunches, jacket potatoes, soup of the day, smoked mackerel pâté, hummus dip with croutons and crispy mushrooms with garlic mayonnaise. More substantial dishes include roast spring chicken with rice and cranberry stuffing, golden scampi with cream cheese dip, grilled gammon with apple and cider sauce,

and grilled sirloin steak. There is a separate board for special dishes of the day. Food is not served on Sunday evening. Apart from the cricket ground, there is a beer garden with provision for children.
Telephone: Trowbridge (0225) 752426.

How to get there: Wingfield is several miles west of Trowbridge, just to the south of the A366. Join the B3109, following the signs for Wingfield. The Poplars is on the right coming from the direction of Trowbridge or Bradford on Avon.

Parking: There is room to park at the Poplars. Wingfield village centre is on the other side of the main B3109. There is limited parking in Church Lane, particularly in the vicinity of the church.

Length of the walk: 3¾ miles. Map: OS Landranger 173 Swindon and Devizes (GR 822567).

Wingfield is a scattered village, much of which is set back from the main B3109 Bradford on Avon road down several narrow lanes well hidden from passing traffic. North of the village, though not on the actual route of the walk, is Midway Manor, once the home of General Shrapnel, the 18th century inventor of the exploding projectile of the same name.

The walk crosses farmland behind the Poplars before running along the bank of the river Frome on the Wiltshire/Somerset border. The scene by the river is quite charming. On the hill above the river there are delightful views across the vale to Somerset. The return leg is a pleasant stroll across farmland.

The Walk
From the pub car park turn left and follow the narrow lane running alongside some cottages. When the lane peters out, go forward onto a drive as waymarked. Follow it to the right of a private garage and continue along between fields and sheep pens. At the next stile, on the right, cross over and bear left. Aim for the stile ahead, then go on to the next one. Go forward to the stile in the field boundary and then out to a lane leading to a farm. Bear left and follow the lane with a line of cottages and houses on the right. As you begin to approach some farm buildings, veer round to the right and then cross the right hand boundary into the field. The path is waymarked. Turn left and follow the field edge, with farm buildings on the left. Keep to the path and follow it round to the right in the field corner. Bear left after a few yards to join a waymarked path crossing a footbridge. Head obliquely left across this field to the stile in the far boundary, set amid the trees and scrub.
Take the path running down between the trees and when it emerges

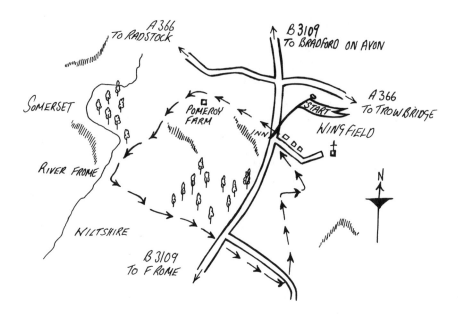

from the woods you are standing on the edge of some watermeadows. Follow the right boundary for a few yards until you reach a stile taking you onto a path running above the fast-flowing river Frome. The river, a tributary of the Avon, represents the county boundary between Wiltshire and Somerset. In time a charming old cottage comes into view over on the Somerset bank, its gardens running down to the water's edge. Rising above it are the houses of Tellisford, a village prettily situated only just within the borders of Somerset. Cross a stile beside an old footbridge. The scene here is most picturesque, and it is worth breaking off from the walk for a few moments in order to stand on the bridge and gaze at the river upstream and down.

Returning to the walk, go up Vagg's Hill away from the Somerset border, noting a footpath on the right to Rode. Pass a cottage, then follow the tarmac lane between banks of trees and bushes. The lane is steep in places. Further on, the lane levels out and in a right hand gateway there are splendid views over to Somerset on the far side of the valley. Pass a footpath on the left and continue. On the right is a turning to Langham Farm. On the left is woodland.

Pass several private properties on the right, and then a farm. The road veers slightly left and soon cuts between fields and hedgerows before reaching the junction. Cross over into Poplar Tree Lane, noting the Somerset border along to the right. Pass Dillybrook Cottage on the right and continue along the road. Glancing back across the fields, there are good views of the trees soaring above the river Frome. Walk past some cottages and when the road veers right, turn sharp left to join a bridleway to Wingfield. Follow the broad bridleway as it runs between hedgerows, trees and bushes. There are fields either side of the way. Further on, the bridleway narrows to a path. Eventually, you reach a junction. Bear right, still on the bridleway. All around you are good views over farmland.

As the bridleway swings right, within sight of a farm, turn left through a gap in the hedge and enter the field. Follow the right hand boundary into the corner, and then in the next corner, where there is a footbridge, cross into the next field. Proceed ahead to the far boundary and join a grassy path beside the garden of a private house. Pass the house and follow the track as far as the B3109 road. At the junction turn right and walk along the verge and then the pavement. Church Lane on the right, leading to Wingfield church and the village centre, is worth exploring. Returning to the B3109, cross it and return to the Poplars car park.

⑲ Horningsham
The Bath Arms

A potted history of the Bath Arms can be found in the entrance lobby. It has been a pub for over 200 years and was originally leased to a man named William Kennell at a rent of £25 for 14 years. How times have changed! At that time it was known as Lord Weymouth's Arms. By the end of the 18th century it was called the Marquess of Bath's Arms. During its history it was also known as the Twelve Apostles. That is the name now given to the groups of lime trees at the front and side of the inn. The stone-built Bath Arms is now a freehouse and hotel. On the walls of the bar are various black and white photographs including Horningsham flower show in 1912. The picture shows village grocer George Chapman having just presented a bouquet to the Marchioness of Bath. There is also an old photograph of Horningsham with the caption, 'On the borders of Somersetshire – 1 mile from Longleat'. Longleat House and the father of the present Marquess of Bath are pictured too.

Food is available seven days a week and includes soup of the day, ploughman's, fresh local trout, homemade curry and open smoked trout sandwich. Wild boar, pheasant and venison are also part of the menu. Fresh fish is a noted speciality. There is a traditional roast on Sundays. Real ale includes Wadworth 6X and Eldridge Pope Dorchester Bitter. There is a dining room (advance booking necessary) with lovely views over towards Longleat Park, and a public bar and skittle alley. Food is served at normal times, while the inn serves drink between 11 in the morning and 11 in the evening from Monday to Saturday. Dogs on a lead please.
Telephone: Warminster (0985) 844308.

How to get there: Horningsham lies on the Wiltshire/Somerset border. From Warminster or Trowbridge follow the A350, then turn right for Horningsham at Longbridge Deverill. From Salisbury follow the A36 and the B3905 to Longbridge Deverill, then continue west.

Parking: You can park at the Bath Arms, or you can park in the village, space permitting.

Length of the walk: 4¼ miles. Map: OS Landranger 183 Yeovil to Frome (GR 809416).

Much of this walk is through Longleat Park, offering excellent views of the great house and its surroundings. Standing in extensive parkland landscaped by Capability Brown in the mid 18th century, Longleat House is a perfect example of Elizabethan architecture. The home of the Thynne family for more than 400 years, it has the distinction of being the first stately home to open to the public. The house includes many fine paintings and artefacts, and possibly the most valuable private library in the world. Outside, there are numerous attractions aimed at the visiting family, including the famous Safari Park. The main house is open every day except 25th December. Between Easter and November there may be a charge for entry into Longleat Park. For further information ring 0985 844551.
The walk heads for the magnificent viewpoint at Heaven's Gate before returning to Horningsham along pleasant field paths and stretches of road. The paths and drives within the boundaries of Longleat Park are not public rights of way, so access to the walk is by kind permission of The Marquess of Bath.

The Walk
From the Bath Arms turn left and head down the lane restricted to one way traffic, following it between holly hedges. Soon you reach a gatehouse and immediately beyond it the magnificent façade of Longleat House comes into view. Proceed down the long straight drive. Note the grazing sheep, and the lake on the right. Just before

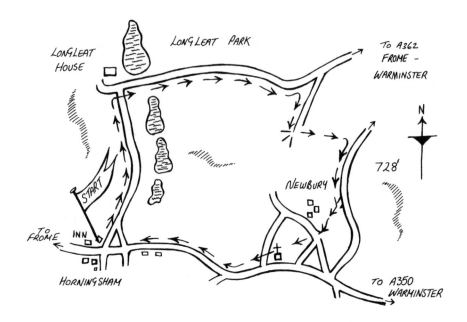

the great house you reach a junction. Turn right and follow the drive. On the right are more grazing sheep and a deer park. Soon the drive begins a gradual ascent and here there are pleasant views over rolling semi-wooded parkland. Pausing to rest at this point, you are treated to a splendid view of Longleat House, and over to the north through the trees there are glimpses of the Safari Park. Follow the drive round a marked bend and continue up the hill, with the Safari Park still visible on the left. Further up, take a sharp right turning to Heaven's Gate. Follow the drive as it runs high above the parkland. Ignore several left hand turnings and eventually you reach the viewpoint at Heaven's Gate, a popular and appropriately named beauty spot. At 400 ft the views from here are outstanding.

Turn left here and beyond the gate join a broad path with lines of tall fir trees and banks of undergrowth. Further on, the wide grassy ride cuts between colourful rhododendron bushes and ornamental trees and shrubs. Follow the path as it bends right to reach the road. Turn right and follow the road edge. After several minutes, when the trees thin, join a track on the right. The track descends to the little village of Newbury. There are good views here over rolling countryside and distant semi-wooded vales.

Join a firm lane and continue as far as the telephone box. Go through the wooden kissing gate and swing half right, keeping parallel to the telegraph poles. Horningsham parish church is visible now. On reaching another kissing gate, go out to the road and turn left. Pass the church of St John the Baptist, occupying a prominent hilltop position. At the road bear right. Longleat House and its parkland are visible through the gaps on the right. Pass Horningsham county primary school. Follow the pavement. On the right along this stretch are several stone-built thatched cottages. Continue along the pavement as it rises above the road. Keeping on the path, with views over undulating countryside, pass the entrance to Mill Farm and cut between various houses and cottages. Eventually, you reach the green at Horningsham. On the far side is the Bath Arms where the walk began.

20 Chitterne
The King's Head

Situated on Salisbury Plain, the King's Head is a Gibbs Mew house and very much a traditional village pub. From the outside it is rather a rambling old stone building, overlooking Chitterne Brook. In winter its customers are mainly local villagers from this quiet little community, or perhaps army personnel from any of the nearby camps. During the summer, however, the pub attracts a wider clientele. Walkers undertaking the Imber Range Perimeter Path, cyclists heading across the plain, and tourists new to the area are among the frequent visitors coming through the front door. The lounge bar and dining area are cosy with a real wood fire in winter. Above the fireplace is a gilt-framed mirror and elsewhere the walls are adorned with decorative china plates and prints of horses and blacksmiths' shops as well as rural scenes of old England. There are various other artefacts and bric a brac. For the games enthusiast the lounge bar has a dartboard, while the public bar includes a pool table.

The menu is simple but appetising with a choice of ploughman's lunches. Beef Madras curry with rice, pork and pineapple casserole, homemade Cornish pasties, battered cod and scampi are among the other dishes available. There is no food on Sunday evenings and no lunchtime roasts during the summer months, the emphasis at this time of the year being more on steaks and salads. There is usually a choice of two real ales in the summer too. Gibbs Mew Timothy Chudley Bitter is a traditional cask ale and very palatable! In winter, Deacon is the other real ale on handpump. There is also Wiltshire Bitter, a keg beer, plus Strongbow Draught Cider and Fosters and Harp lager. Outside, there is a beer garden. The King's Head, which also does bed and breakfast, is a straightforward, unpretentious local inn with a simple homely charm.

Telephone: Warminster (0985) 50269.

How to get there: Chitterne lies on the southern edge of Salisbury Plain, on the B390 Heytesbury to Shrewton road. It is in remote country, the nearest town of any size being Warminster. The inn is at the western end of the village.

Parking: There is a car park at the King's Head, or you may find space to park in the vicinity of Chitterne church.

Length of the walk: 6 miles. Map: OS Landranger 184 Salisbury and the Plain (GR 988438).

When you think of the Plain the image that comes to mind tends to be of an undulating chalk plateau, a hostile, desolate place with much evidence of military activity and a tangible air of ancient mystery. Salisbury Plain and the whole of North Wessex were once the most heavily populated areas in the country, inhabited by the people of the late Stone Age and Bronze Age. Ironically, today, in this overcrowded island of ours, the Plain is one of the loneliest and least populated tracts of land in the south of England, if not all of Britain.

The walk proves most effectively that there are a number of rights of way criss-crossing Salisbury Plain, providing access, albeit limited, to this austere landscape. However, the route is open and exposed with few opportunities to shelter from the wind and rain. When weather conditions are not as good as they could be, it is a walk ideally suited perhaps to the more adventurous rambler, but on a sunny spring day, the surroundings are never less than spectacular.

The Walk

From the front of the King's Head turn right and follow the road, with the Chitterne Brook in the fields over on the left. The brook is a 'winter bourne'. Dry in summer, the channel runs through the centre of the village. Pass some farm buildings on the right. Where the road bends left, turn right to join a waymarked path running between trees and bushes. This is part of the Imber Range Perimeter Path, a 30 mile circular walk following the outer boundary of the military firing and

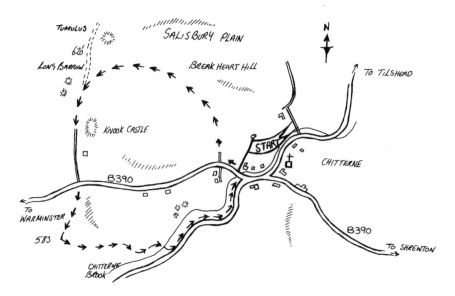

training area.

Follow the sunken bridleway and, when the trees thin out, there are views over fields either side of the route. Glancing back at intervals reveals magnificent far-reaching views across the southern edge of the Plain. The views to the south are the best, as you gaze out over a wide landscape of open chalk downland, dotted with belts of woodland, stretching down to the Wylye valley. On these grassy slopes the only sounds you are likely to hear are the booms and bangs of the army, and perhaps a skylark swooping overhead.

Pass over a crosstrack and continue. Go through a small copse and keep to the grassy track. As you head over Breakheart Hill, you will see the MOD ranges on the right. It is important to keep to the Imber Range Path, ensuring that you do not trespass beyond the warning notices. When you reach a junction of paths, veer left and continue along the Imber Range Path. Avoid a turning down to a small copse enclosing some farm buildings and continue up the slope to another junction where there is a byway on the left. This is the start of the next stage of the walk. However, on a clear day it is worth continuing along the track for several minutes until it begins to descend the slope. At this point, 600 ft above sea level, you can see a range of distant rounded hills, including Cotley Hill, Battlesbury Hill and Scratchbury Hill. There are good views to the north across the heart of Salisbury Plain. The 360° views from here are so extensive that when visibility is good you can probably see up to 15 miles or more. Beside the path there are the remains of various barrows and tumuli.

Return to the byway and follow it in a southerly direction towards some farm buildings. On the left of the track is visible evidence of Knook Castle and its ancient remains. The old ramparts and ditches are now little more than just lumpy grassy mounds. Pass the farm and continue down to the B390 Chitterne – Heytesbury road. Cross the road to a byway. Follow it with light woodland on the left. There are spectacular views to the west towards Heytesbury, where the First World War poet Siegfried Sassoon lived until his death in 1967, having earlier been stationed locally.

Pass a corrugated barn and after about 120 yards swing left to join a waymarked track. On the left among the trees is the outline of Upton Great Barrow. This homeward stretch of the walk is over civilian-owned land, the army ranges being to the north of the B390. When the track bends left, continue ahead along the left boundary of a field. After about 50 yards bear left into the adjacent field and continue in the same direction with the fence on the right. Over to the right lies the Wylye valley, with extensive wooded slopes rising up beyond it. In the foreground are good views of rolling downland and plantations of regimented trees. In the field corner go through a gate and turn left for a few yards to a gate post. Bear right and keep the fence on the left as you cross the high windswept downs. Eventually, you reach the field corner and crossing a stile, bear right to continue down the slopes, keeping the fence on the right. At the fence corner turn right to the next corner, then swing left and go down to a farm track with a line of fir trees on the right. There are good views of downland with Chitterne Brook winding through the valley below.

Turn left and follow the metalled track. The scenery changes quite significantly in character as the landscape becomes softer and less hostile than the bare downland of earlier. Go along the track until you draw level with the brook. Turn right at this point to join a waymarked riverside path. Ignore the first bridge and go on for a few yards to the second one. Cross it and go straight ahead to a double stile in the far boundary, then on across the next field to another stile where you join the road. Bear left and walk back to the King's Head in the village.

㉑ Stourton
The Spread Eagle Inn

The Spread Eagle has been in regular use over two centuries. Originally, it was known as the 'Stourton Inn' and then the 'Eagle Arms Inn'. It has always been part of the Stourhead estate, being one of the gifts made over to the National Trust in 1947. Undoubtedly, it is a handsome building consisting of Flemish bond brickwork, Georgian and Regency fireplaces and some 18th century doorcases. Beneath the inn are barrel vaulted beer and wine cellars. Many alterations have taken place here over the years. According to a short written history of the Spread Eagle, a number of distinguished visitors have passed through its doors, Horace Walpole and David Niven among them. The Spread Eagle is very popular with visitors to Stourhead and has a dignified air about it, with the stamp of the National Trust quite evident.

Bar meals are available every day and include homemade soup, ploughman's with a tempting choice of local mature cheddar or Somerset brie. More substantial meals include local cooked cold gammon ham, homemade steak and ale pie, lean beef cooked in a locally brewed ale and topped with a puff pastry lid, homemade mushroom stroganoff and various daily specials from the board, including scampi and chips and tuna bake, with a traditional Sunday roast in winter. There is a choice of desserts and children's portions of most items. Thick handled cutlery, high chairs and bottle-warming facilities are supplied if required!

Charringtons Bass and Ash Vine Bitter are the permanent real ales and there is Tetley Keg Bitter, and Dry Blackthorn Cider. The bar and dining areas are spacious and roomy with black and white photographs of Kilmington and Stourton cricket club, and various trophies. There are also log fires in season. During the winter, from October to April, the Spread Eagle is open for morning coffee and in the afternoon for tea and drinks. There is pure Assam tea, freshly brewed coffee and a special cream tea comprising tea, two scones, jam and cream, toasted teacake, buttered crumpet or toast. A perfect end to a walk in the country! The Spread Eagle also does accommodation. Telephone: Bourton (0747) 840587.

How to get there: Stourton is on the Wiltshire/Somerset boundary, to the north of the A303, just off the B3092 Frome road.

Parking: There is a car park at the Spread Eagle Inn. Alternatively, if you plan to visit Stourhead House or garden (the house is open between April and October daily except Thursday and Friday, the garden all year round) you could use the car park there.

Length of the walk: 5 miles. Map: OS Landranger 183 Yeovil to Frome (GR 776338).

The landscape gardens at Stourhead, where this walk begins, are regarded as among the finest in the country – and rightly so. The lakes, which date from 1448, temples, shrubs and rare trees feature in countless books, calendars and postcards.

From the National Trust site at Stourton, the route crosses the Stourhead estate on which there are 1100 acres of woodland. The walk is tranquil here, passing between endless rows of trees. At length the path reaches Alfred's Tower, a famous folly built in 1772. From here you return to the Stourhead estate for the final leg of the walk.

The Walk
Leave the inn, bear left and pass Stourton post office and stores and the entrance to Stourhead gardens. The river Stour rises here. The gardens were designed and laid out by Henry Hoare in the 18th century. Buildings here include the Pantheon and the Temple of Flora, two examples of architecture at its most graceful. The lake is a picture with its banks of trees. Just beside the road is the medieval Bristol High Cross. Originally, it stood in the centre of Bristol before being moved

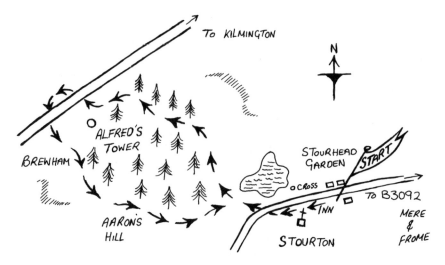

to Stourhead in 1765. The upper and lower niches contain statues of King John, Henry III, Edward III and Henry VI among others.

Follow the road and on the right are good glimpses of the tree-fringed lake. Pass through a stone arch and then turn right (public footpath to Alfred's Tower). A few yards down the track reveals an expanse of water on the left. An old waterwheel and a spectacular cascading waterfall can be seen at this point. Continue along the track as it cuts through the Stourhead estate. Pass a stone cottage set back from the track, on the edge of the trees. On the far horizon the outline of Alfred's Tower can be glimpsed.

Go through a gate which has an accompanying stile. When the track forks, veer right (signposted 'Alfred's Tower'). Go over another stile and continue to follow the track, along which clusters of snowdrops can be seen in late winter. Pass a National Trust sign and continue through the trees, with clearings now and again where trees have been felled. Most of the estate is growing productive timber. There are nature trails through the forest, which is the home of badgers, foxes and roe deer and over 100 species of bird, buzzards, long-eared owls and nightingales among them. The track begins to climb through the woods, becoming progressively steeper. Looking back provides a pleasant vista down through the forest. Further on, you reach a muddy track. Bear left here and head towards Alfred's Tower. Walk along the broad track and shortly a splendid tree-framed vista of the triangular folly opens up in front of you. The red brick tower is 160 ft high and is considered one of the finest in the country. The windowless structure was built for the impressive view from the top, and to mark the spot where Alfred the Great erected his standard against Danish invaders in AD 879. There is a statue of Alfred depicted looking out over a landscape now cloaked with trees and a faded plaque can be seen above the main door. The spire, hit by an aircraft in World War II, was eventually replaced in 1985. The tower is open from 1st April until 1st November daily, except Friday and Monday, 2 pm to 5.30 pm or dusk if earlier.

Make for the exit out to the road and turn left. You are now in Somerset. Follow the lane between banks of trees. Pass the village sign for Brewham and go down until you reach a path veering off to the left. This is part of the Leland Trail, which starts at Alfred's Tower. The route is named after John Leland, the 16th century scholar and antiquarian who spent much of his time travelling the countryside on horseback. He was engaged by Henry VIII as keeper of the royal library, a post he held until 1530. The trail, which is 28 miles long, finishing at Ham Hill country park near Yeovil, is not the precise route Leland chose, more a romantic interpretation of his journey. Further details on it can be obtained from South Somerset District Council in Yeovil.

On the right here are glorious views over east Somerset. Join the Leland Trail, heading towards Aaron's Hill. Avoid a bridle path on the left. The trail is well waymarked. When it forks, bear left and head down the muddy bank. On reaching a track, swing left and follow it as it crosses the wooded slopes of the Stourhead estate. Proceed over a crosstrack and continue to wind between woodland and undergrowth. At length, on reaching a junction, veer right. Avoid turnings either side. Gradually, an open expanse of parkland comes into view, with forest slopes rising in the distance. Go through a wooden gate and follow a grassy track across the parkland. Over to the left here are splendid views of the Stourhead estate. Nestling among the trees is The Convent, an irregular rustic building designed in Gothic style with turrets and spires and built between 1760 and 1770. It is now a private house.

Pass through a gate and follow the track between banks of trees and holly bushes. Cross a fast-flowing stream running beneath the track. Beyond another gate you join a track and it is at this point that you rejoin the earlier path. Retrace your steps to the Spread Eagle.

22 East Knoyle
The Seymour Arms

The inn is 17th century and is named after the Seymour family who once owned part of the village. During the summer, the walls of the pub are covered with virginia creeper. Inside, it is bright and welcoming with an open-plan lounge and public bar area. There is a dining area at one end of the lounge, and a separate dining room. The decor is attractive, with part brick and part panelled walls, beams and wall lights, traditional pub chairs and tables and some high backed bench seats. Scattered around are artefacts including various jugs and old keys. Accommodation is available.

This is a Wadworth house and the real ales include Wadworth 6X and Henry's IPA. There is Dry Blackthorn Cider, Carlsberg, Stella Artois and Toby keg. Food is available every day though not on Monday evenings in winter. During the summer, between July and September, the inn is open from 11 in the morning until 11 at night. An extensive menu includes a range of daily specials. Among the starters are soup of the day, breaded mushrooms and prawn cocktail. There is a choice of jacket potatoes and ploughman's. Main courses include 16 oz T-bone steak, steak Diane in a cream, brandy and

mushroom sauce, mixed grill, chicken Kiev and turkey escalope. Vegetarian dishes include spinach and mushroom lasagne, and vegetable samosa. There is a selection of sweets and a children's menu. Children are welcome in the dining room and dining area and in the beer garden. No dogs please.
Telephone: East Knoyle (0747) 830374.

How to get there: East Knoyle is on the A350 between Warminster and Shaftesbury. The Seymour Arms is on the main road, at the southern end of the village.

Parking: There is a car park at the Seymour Arms. Alternatively, there should be room to park in the road by the church, or close to Wren's shop and post office.

Length of the walk: 4 miles. Map: OS Landranger 183 Yeovil to Frome (GR 882302).

East Knoyle is a large scattered village on a greensand ridge surrounded by fine walking country. Christopher Wren, whose father was Rector at East Knoyle, was born in a room above the village shop in October 1632. The walk meanders round the village boundaries for a while before passing through several charming hamlets on its way to the top of Windmill Hill. From here there are superb views over the Blackmoor Vale. There are several sections of road walking, along quiet country lanes. However, jets from nearby RAF Yeovilton may enliven the peace and quiet of the countryside from time to time!

The Walk
Take the path at the back of the pub, passing through the gate to join a waymarked path. Go straight across the field to the gate in the hedge. Over to the left are very good views of East Knoyle, with the church tower visible among the trees on the hillside and groups of cottages gathered in higgledy-piggledy fashion around it. On reaching the road, bear left towards East Knoyle. After about 100 yards turn right to join another waymarked path, following it beside a pond on the left. When you reach a wide grassy ride, head diagonally left to a stile in the boundary fence. Cross a small plantation to another stile, then veer diagonally right to the far corner of the field. A stile takes you out to join the ride you crossed minutes earlier. Turn right for a few steps, then left to join a muddy path running beneath the trees. Pass under a stone bridge built by the original owners of nearby Clouds House as part of a carriage drive.

The path descends quite steeply under the trees and there is a field on the right fringed by woodland. Soon the path widens to a track before reaching the road. Turn left and follow the road between high hedgerows. Pass Park Farm and when you reach the main A350, cross over and go through the wrought iron kissing gate. Veer obliquely right and aim for another gate in the right corner of the field, noting a small enclosure containing a newly planted tree beneath which is the inscription: '1992 – in memory of Mum and Dad'.

Cross a drive leading to Clouds House and join a waymarked path, continuing ahead across a paddock with the grounds of Clouds House on the left. This was built for the Wyndham family in 1886, but burnt to the ground soon afterwards. 'Clouds', appropriately named in view of its hilltop position, was completely rebuilt in 1893.

When you reach a stile leading you out to the road, bear left and follow the lane between high hedges and trees down to some charming stone houses at the junction. Turn left and at the next junction, near a telephone box, bear right. This is Milton, a peaceful hamlet of houses and cottages. When the houses peter out, swing left over a stile and then aim half right, up the field. Looking back, on these grassy slopes, there is a delightful vista of Milton with steeply rising wooded hills beyond. It is a picture so typically English in both beauty and character that it could almost come straight from the pages of a calendar or the lid of a biscuit tin.

Pass through the gap into the next field, climbing steeply. When the ground levels out, proceed ahead to the far boundary and go out to the road. Turn left and follow the lane down to the T junction at The Green, another tiny settlement on the outskirts of East Knoyle. Bear right for a few yards and then left opposite The Fox and Hounds where there is a striking view across the Blackmoor Vale. Head across the grass, keeping the view on the right. Follow the path between lines of trees and scrub. Ignore a branch path to the right and continue ahead on the higher path. Further on, there is a major junction, with a path on the right, a path straight ahead and a path veering to the left. Take the latter route and follow it over a wooded plateau, continuing to swing left. Ignore the sunken path below. Between the trees on the right are magnificent and memorable views of the Blackmoor Vale – a vast green patchwork stretching to the horizon.

Soon the trees thin to reveal even more spectacular views. You are now on top of Windmill Hill, 650 ft above sea level. If time permits, you may like to continue to the road in order to look at the old stone windmill on the opposite side. Retrace your steps along the path towards The Fox and Hounds for a short distance. As you approach the point where the trees on the left begin to obscure the views, veer over to the left and look for a thin bridle path cutting down the bank. This is so narrow and restricted in places you wonder how on earth a horse could negotiate such a hazardous passage. The views are

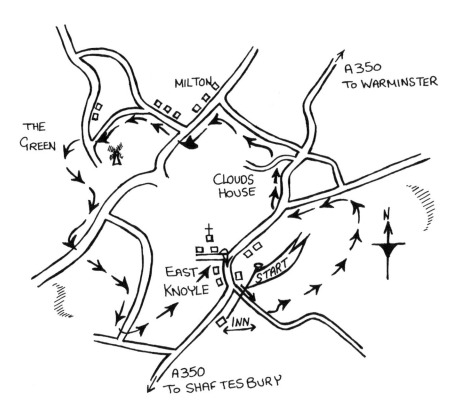

constant and unchanging as you make your way down to the road at Underhill.

Turn right and follow the road towards Mere. Some way down you reach Brickyard Farm. Bear left here to join a waymarked path running alongside some paddocks. Go through a gate and down past a couple of small lakes which can be seen from the top of Windmill Hill. Pass through another gate and descend the slope to the next gate. Go through it and then straight ahead following the field boundary, keeping the fence on your immediate right. In the top boundary go through the gate into the next field. Follow the line of trees along the right boundary and when you reach a wooden fence enclosing the grounds of a large stone house, continue as far as the stile.

Head out onto the drive, turn left and make for the road at Holloway. At the junction bear right opposite The Old Rectory. After a few yards bear right into Holloway Lane, signposted 'Semley and Shaftesbury'. There are various houses and fields on the right and a sizeable area of woodland on the left. When the road bends right, swing sharp left into a field. Head across the open field towards the houses of East Knoyle, keeping the woodland on the left at all times. Gradually, the field tapers, the houses of the village growing ever nearer. Go through a gate into a paddock with the church easily seen through a splendid vista. Join a hard path and continue to the road opposite the church. Glancing back as you reach the gate reveals an impressive view of East Knoyle with the hills circling the village like protective guardians.

Turn right and go along to the junction in the village centre. A plaque commemorating Christopher Wren's birthplace can be seen here. His family occupied the premises at the time of his birth as there had been a fire at the rectory.

The land on the far side of the road was purchased by the people of the village in 1975 as an open space for exercise and recreation. Bear right at the junction and walk down the main street of the village, taking special care where there is no pavement. Take the lane on the left signposted 'West Tisbury' and follow it as far as the waymarked path on the right. Join the path and retrace your steps to the Seymour Arms.

㉓ Fonthill Bishop
The King's Arms

Before it was a public house, the King's Arms was simply a barn. Part of it still remains to this day – you can see it clinging to the hillside at the back. The original outside wall of the barn can be seen inside the pub, forming the back wall of the games area. The building was extended and rebuilt in about 1850. It is the only freehold building in the estate village of Fonthill Bishop. The landlord has been in the trade for many years. He's quite a character, a bit of a wag. He presides over the place, smoking his cigars and talking light-heartedly about pre-decimal pounds, shillings and pence!

Bar food includes ploughman's platter, pâté and toast, a range of jacket potatoes, Horseman's Special comprising jumbo sausages, bacon, egg, baked beans and chips, cold Wiltshire ham, chicken and chips, fillet of breaded haddock, 8 oz rump steak and roast chicken quarter. There is also the King's Ransom which is a 10 oz sirloin steak in garlic butter and various homemade dishes including steak and kidney pie and vegetable curry with rice. A traditional roast is available on Sunday. Real ales include Wadworth 6X, Flowers Original and Strong Country Bitter. There is Strongbow Cider, Stella Artois and

Murphy's Irish Stout. Children are welcome in the dining area and the garden, as are well behaved dogs. The King's Arms, which also does accommodation, is a freehouse.

Telephone: Hindon (0747) 89523.

How to get there: Fonthill Bishop, near Hindon, is on the B3089 Mere road, about 1 mile south of the A303. The King's Arms is at the eastern end of the village, on the main road.

Parking: You can easily park at the inn. Alternatively, there are some spaces in the village centre, in the area surrounding the church and shop.

Length of the walk: 4 miles. Map: OS Landranger 184 Salisbury and the Plain (GR 936328).

This walk offers the chance to explore some of the prettiest countryside in this part of Wiltshire. To begin with, it crosses level farmland near Fonthill Bishop, and later it passes close to the site of Fonthill Abbey where, in the 18th century, the eccentric millionaire and author, William Beckford, attempted to build an extravagant 'Gothic dream palace'.

The final leg of the walk hugs the shores of a large lake in Fonthill Park, providing most attractive glimpses of the water through the trees. As you approach the end of the walk, you pass through the splendid arched gateway to the park, attributed to Inigo Jones.

The Walk

From the inn car park turn left and walk down the B3089 towards the centre of Fonthill Bishop, passing a turning to Wylye and Warminster. Swing right and enter the churchyard. Follow the gravel path as far as the field boundary. Go through a kissing gate and continue ahead along the left boundary of the field. On the left now is a good view of the arched gateway through which we pass at the end of this highly enjoyable walk. Head for the field corner where there is a stile and continue across the next field to a stile, with a cottage down to the left. Aim for a gate and a line of stone cottages up ahead.

Go through a gate to join a lane running alongside the cottages towards Berwick St Leonard, an agricultural hamlet where William of Orange spent a night in 1688 prior to taking the throne. As the lane bends left, note the church on the right. Follow the lane to the road (B3089), turn right and then almost immediately left to join a bridleway. Follow the field boundary. Looking back reveals a broad sweep of farmland and downland. Down below are the buildings of Berwick St Leonard.

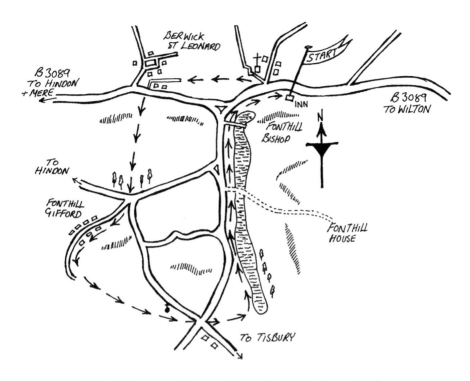

Proceed ahead for some distance along the field edge and when you reach some woodland, go through a gate into the trees. Follow the path, avoiding branch turnings. It descends through the woods to a junction with a 'private-keep out' sign on the left. Go on down the bank and along the edge of a vegetable garden. Bear right in the corner and join a track running along the front of some stone cottages. At the junction turn left and proceed to the road. Bear left and walk down almost to the point where it swings right. Veer right along a 'no through road'.

This is Fonthill Gifford. There is evidence here that this, like Fonthill Bishop, was built as an estate village to form part of the huge Fonthill estate. In the park the Marquis of Westminster built a Scottish baronial-style mansion. He also rebuilt the church. Pass some cottages and continue onto a track running deep into the countryside. Later, you cut between several houses either side of the route. Continue for a short distance until you reach a waymarked footpath on the left. Join the path and note the good views of the houses at Fonthill Gifford. Cross the field by heading diagonally right and aiming for a clear waymarked track running along the perimeter of the field. In the top right corner cross into the next field. Go forward and keep the boundary on the right. Carry on towards the church steeple at Fonthill Gifford. Eventually you join a track. Pass a vineyard on the left.

Walk down between various farm buildings and animal pens to reach the road. Turn right and pass the imposing edifice of the Beckford Arms on the right. Less than a mile away to the west are the remains of Fonthill Abbey, built in the late 18th century by William Beckford and described by Pevsner as 'his great Gothic folly'. The scale of the plan was such that the Abbey tower was intended to be as high as St Paul's Cathedral. Beckford built in a terrible hurry, employing 500 men to work day and night and keeping fires burning to prevent plaster and cement from freezing. He even entertained Nelson and Lady Hamilton here for Christmas. Eventually, in 1823, Beckford abandoned the place and moved to Bath, his ambitious plans having proved too much. The Abbey collapsed several years after his departure.

Follow the Tisbury/Hindon road for a short distance and then bear left to join a straight waymarked track cutting between fields down to the edge of a large lake set in private parkland. The descent provides very good views of the water and the wooded banks on the far side. Go through a gate marked 'private' (there is a yellow public footpath sign indicating this is a right of way).

At the water's edge swing sharp left to join a semi-wooded path, with constant views of the lake on the right. Not surprisingly, this is a popular spot and the path often becomes crowded along here. It also gets muddy after heavy rain. Continue between the trees and eventually you join the road. Proceed towards Fonthill Bishop with the lake still visible on the right. Up ahead is the magnificent arched gateway beyond which is a fork in the road. Veer right to join the B3089 in the centre of the village. Pass the post office and stores and walk along the road to the inn car park.

24 Berwick St John
The Talbot

Located in the Ebble valley, the Talbot is a delightful and extremely popular village inn in the centre of this most attractive village. Built in 1540, the Talbot has been a pub for about 200 years. It consists of one single long bar with window seats, heavy black beams and cross beams, and an inglenook fireplace with iron fireback and bread ovens. There is also an old black and white photograph of the local blacksmith, taken in 1912. Next door is a panelled dining area which also includes old photographs.

The inn has a good reputation for food in the area and a wide selection of dishes is available every day except Sunday. The lunchtime menu includes chicken curry, cold beef or ham platter, ocean delight – an appetizing combination of prawns and crabsticks in a cocktail dressing topped with lemon. Basket meals include scampi and southern style king prawns and there are ploughman's and jacket potatoes. The evening menu has a choice of starters, with main dishes including lasagne, macaroni au gratin, ham, egg and chips, and T-bone steak. Jacket potatoes and basket meals are the same as lunchtime. From the board you can choose fresh trout, steak and kidney pie, game pie or beef curry. Four real ales are on offer – Wadworth 6X,

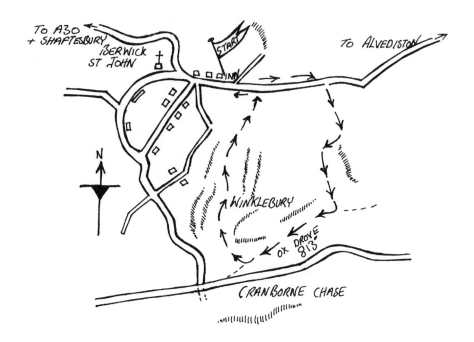

Badger Best, Adnams and Bass. There is also draught Guinness and sweet and dry cider. It is advisable to book for food. Dogs are not permitted in the pub but there is an enclosed garden at the rear, which also caters for children. Note the seat 'Donated by the many friends of Eva, 1911-91, who sadly miss her warmth, wit and charm at the Talbot Inn'.

Telephone: Shaftesbury (0747) 828222.

How to get there: Berwick St John is just to the south of the A30, near Shaftesbury. The village and the inn are both signposted from the main road.

Parking: There is a car park at the inn. The landlord operates a security system so it is advisable to ring him in advance if you want to leave a car here when the pub is not open for business. Alternatively, you could park in the village itself or its outskirts where there are some spaces.

Length of the walk: 3½ miles. Map: OS Landranger 184 Salisbury and the Plain (GR 947224).

Situated deep in hill country on the Wiltshire/Dorset borders, Berwick St John is a delightful village nestling in the shadow of Cranborne Chase, a favourite hunting ground of King John. The village boasts a charming tale of an ancient custom dating back more than 200 years. A kindly rector, whose parish this was, stipulated in his will that the church bell must be rung for 15 minutes at eight o'clock every night in winter in order to help travellers who may have become lost in the surrounding hills.

The walk climbs high above the village, where there are spectacular views down the Ebble valley and west towards Shaftesbury, and then returns by way of Winklebury Hill, the site of an Iron Age fort and a Saxon burial ground.

The Walk

From the car park turn left, cross the stream and walk along the road beside several picturesque cottages and a large stone-built house. Pass a track in the left bank, signposted 'Woodlands'. There are good views to the right of Winklebury Hill rising up towards Cranborne Chase. Proceed beyond several cottages and a bungalow, continuing along the road until you reach a pair of semi-detached houses. Turn right onto a bridleway heading towards Lower Bridmore Farm. Here you are in a rumpled undulating landscape of spectacular hilltops and wooded downland. The track approaches a pond and then reaches the stone farm buildings. Follow the bridleway as it continues beyond the farm and climbs steadily between banks of trees.

The track becomes grassy further up, the banks giving way to reveal good open views either side of you. On the grassy slopes of the downs bear left and follow the bridleway through several fields, heading for a line of trees. On reaching the trees bear right and walk along Ox Drove on the northern fringes of Cranborne Chase. This is an old drovers' road across the downs. The views from here are stunning. Continue with light woodland on the left. At length, just before the road, you reach a bridleway on the right. Take the turning and follow it between wire fences. Avoid the stile and footpath on the left and stay on the main bridleway. The path begins to narrow and on the right are views of rolling partly wooded countryside. The route of the walk descends gradually over the slopes of Winklebury Hill, becoming more sunken as it cuts between high banks of trees. Being a bridleway, the path can become wet and muddy underfoot. On reaching a junction bear left. At this point in a gap in the trees is a fine downland view which is worth pausing to admire and Lower Bridmore Farm, encountered earlier in the walk, can be seen from here. Follow the bridleway between lines of trees and banks of ivy and undergrowth. At the road turn left and return to the Talbot.

② Fovant
The Cross Keys

A rambling, stone-built pub, the Cross Keys is full of nooks and crannies. It was built in 1485 and subsequently became a coaching inn. The area was once a noted haunt of highwaymen and you can read about one colourful robber in an old newspaper cutting on display in the bar. During its long history, the Cross Keys has seen many internal changes. An old stable has become a bar and what used to be the kitchen is now a restaurant. Earlier this century the inn witnessed much activity in the village street, when, during the First World War, King George V inspected the troops at Fovant. There is a photograph of the King standing outside the Cross Keys at the time.

Several real ales are on offer, Wadworth 6X and Adnams Southwold Bitter among them. Dry Blackthorn Cider and Carlsberg Export and

Pilsner are also available. There is a good range of food to choose from, with mixed grill, T-bone steak, 8 oz English rump steak, breaded plaice and cottage pie among the dishes. There are also vegetarian meals including broccoli and cream cheese pie and vegetarian curry and rice. The selection of light snacks includes ham salad, chicken salad, ploughman's and toasted steak, ham or cheese. Dishes on the children's menu include cheeseburger in a roll and salad. There is also a selection of sweets including apple tart and raspberry mousse. On Sundays there is a traditional roast. The Cross Keys also does accommodation, afternoon tea and morning coffee. Dogs may not join you inside.

Telephone: Fovant (0722) 714284.

How to get there: Fovant is midway between Salisbury and Shaftesbury, on the A30 London-Exeter road.

Parking: There is a car park at the side of the Cross Keys and some spaces in the road to Chilmark, opposite the inn.

Length of the walk: 3 miles. Map: OS Landranger 184 Salisbury and the Plain (GR 006285).

This is a walk circumnavigating the regimental badges cut into the chalk downs above Fovant, a village of picturesque stone cottages straddling the A30. During the First World War there was a training camp at Fovant and thousands of servicemen from all over the world, many of them members of the Australian Infantry, congregated here before departing for the Western Front. They carved the badges of their regiments into the chalk in their spare time, starting in 1916. The camp was extensive, overwhelming the village with its rifle ranges, parade grounds, hospitals and railway. At certain times of the year, from the air, the outline of the old camp can still be identified and, on the downs, the badges serve as a constant memorial to the skill and dedication of the men who were stationed there. This is quite a short walk with a steep climb to the summit of the downs, the slope being 1 in 4. The views from the top are magnificent and you can look right across the Nadder valley towards the edge of Salisbury Plain.

The Walk

From the car park turn left and walk down the main street (A30). Immediately past the inn, veer left onto a narrow back lane cutting between some houses. Continue ahead when the lane bends right to reach the main road. The track is rougher now. Further along, on the outskirts of Fovant, it swings sharp left. Over to the right along this stretch of the walk are excellent views of the badges cut into the hillside. Among the insignias carved were those of The 6th City of

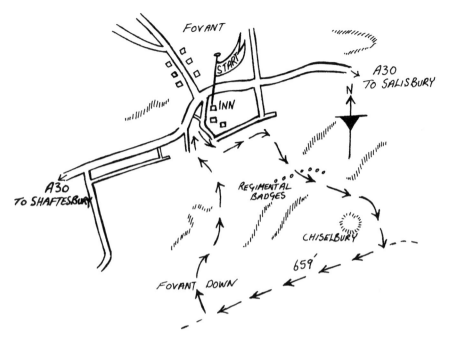

London Regiment, The Wiltshire Regiment, The Devonshire Regiment, The Post Office Rifles and The Young Men's Christian Association. Maintenance and preservation is carried out voluntarily by the Fovant Badges Society.

Head towards East Farm. Draw level with the house and buildings, then bear right to join a signposted path heading for the hill. Go through the gate and walk along the field edge towards the steep slopes. In the field corner cross a stile and veer half left following a clear, chalky path as it ascends the hillside in dramatic fashion. It is certainly a steep climb, but stopping at regular intervals provides the opportunity to study the spectacular views, as well as catch your breath! Fovant can easily be seen from here, and the Nadder valley beyond. The insignias are best appreciated from a distance. Close up they are nothing more than lines and squares of stones and chalk incisions forming intricate patterns on the grassy hillside.

Follow the thin scar across the slopes and soon a wire fence comes into view on the right. Look for a stile. Once over it, go forward and take the path round the eastern edge of the hillfort. On reaching a track bear right. This is one of the old sheep droves running between Salisbury Racecourse and Shaftesbury. Keep on the track as it cuts between hedgerows and light woodland. Avoid a waymarked path on

107

the right and proceed to the next right hand path where a sign advises you to keep dogs on a lead. Take this path and follow it between gorse, trees and brambles. Soon there are magnificent views once again over towards Fovant and the Nadder valley. Look for a clear grassy path on the right further down. Take the path and go down to a stile. Beyond it you cut between brambles and undergrowth before emerging into the corner of a large field. Proceed ahead along the field edge towards the buildings of Fovant. The badges come into view over to the right. Eventually you reach a stile. Go forward to the next stile. Cross it to join the track on a sharp bend and continue straight ahead. Retrace your steps back to the Cross Keys in the centre of Fovant.

26 **Barford St Martin**
The Barford Inn

The Barford Inn used to be called the Green Dragon. Built as a coaching inn and brewery which served pubs within an 8 mile radius up until about the turn of the century, it is situated in the heart of the village, on a corner of the A30. Inside, there are various alcoves and recesses, artefacts with a rural theme, stone walls, beams, a copper kettle, and some black and white photographs of how the inn used to look. There is dark squared oak panelling and bench seats, and on one wall is a glass case containing clay pipe designs. One bowl bears the head of Field Marshal Lord Kitchener, another a bearded negro. Outside, there is no garden but a quaint old courtyard at the front.

The inn is a restaurant pub and good food is its speciality (booking is advisable at weekends). The menu is divided into distinct categories.

Starters or 'light bites' include a large bowl of homemade soup, rollmop herring, Barford prawn platter, chicken liver pâté, corn on the cob and locally smoked salmon. Ploughman's lunches include Wiltshire ham, ripe Cheddar and Stilton. There are cold platters, savoury jacket potatoes, vegetarian suggestions, including macaroni cheese and tagliatelli provençale, 'fish delights' including salmon steak and deep fried plaice, and 'popular poultry' with curried chicken and chicken tikka masala. The mouthwatering meat dishes include grilled sirloin steak and Cumberland sausages. There is a selection of sweets from the display cabinet. The real ale on handpump is Badger Best, Dry Blackthorn Cider and Munchener Pilsner Lager are also available. One bar is reserved for non smokers. Families are welcome. Telephone: Salisbury (0722) 742242.

How to get there: Barford St Martin is a pleasant village lying on a sharp bend of the A30. From Salisbury follow the signs for Wilton and then continue along the A30 to reach the village. The Barford Inn is on the right on the bend.

Parking: There is a huge car park at the rear of the Barford Inn. Alternatively, you could park outside the church, near the junction of Factory Lane and Duck Lane.

Length of the walk: 4 miles. Map: OS Landranger 184 Salisbury and the Plain (GR 056314).

My abiding memory of this splendid walk is the extraordinarily isolated tract of wooded countryside to the north of the village of Barford St Martin. It is difficult enough these days to escape the constant reminders of the stressful late 20th century, and the ever encroaching congestion of the south of England, but to my mind this walk manages to transport the country lover to a secret undisturbed world of silent woodland and quiet paths. Only an occasional military helicopter disturbs the calm! It is tailor-made for those who want to get away from it all.

The Walk
From the car park turn right to the junction. Avoid the busy A30 and bear left along the 'No Through Road'. Pass through the railway arch and continue with farm buildings on the right. Follow the lane round several bends, avoiding a bridleway on the right. Proceed along the main track as the surface becomes rougher underfoot. Quite quickly you arrive at a junction of tracks. Turn right and follow the bridleway as it cuts deeper into this remote lonely country. The track continues an upward pull, and looking behind you to the south there are impressive views over rolling downland. Follow the track into the

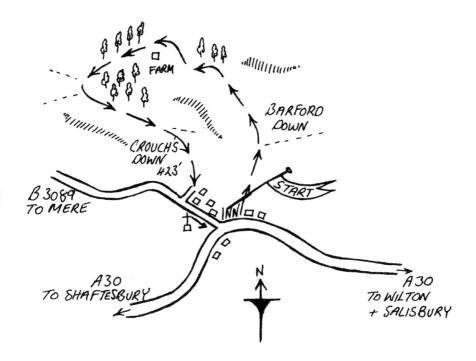

trees of Grovely Wood, during the Middle Ages one of the nine royal forests in Wiltshire. On 29th May each year, Oak Apple Day, an old custom, which is associated with pre-Christian tree worship, permits villagers from nearby Great Wishford to gather fallen and dead wood from Grovely Wood. Originally, this tradition extended to other villages, Barford St Martin among them. The custom still includes a ritual ceremony which involves villagers processing to Salisbury Cathedral where, at the steps of the high altar, they proclaim their rights, chanting 'Grovely! Grovely! and all Grovely! Unity is strength'.

Join a track running sharp left and follow it between the trees. In a couple of minutes you come to a junction with glimpses of a field ahead. Bear right here and follow the green lane towards Grovely Farm. There are good views on the left over to distant ridges on the southerly horizon. When you reach the farm, proceed ahead. After about 100 yards the route swings left just before an old ruined house.

Follow the bridleway as it skirts the fringe of some woodland. In due course the track emerges from the trees and cuts between fields. After several minutes you reach a major junction of tracks and paths. Bear left here. Follow the track between fences with good downland views to the right over towards the Nadder valley. Behind you, too,

111

are striking views towards distant woodland. Ignore a gateway on the right and continue ahead, with woodland on the left. Follow the grassy track down the slope and up the other side. Soon the view ahead widens as you begin to descend the hillside. A line of telegraph poles can be seen marching out across the landscape.

Some way down the slope, look for a gap in the right hand fence. Pass through the gap and follow the waymarked footpath as it runs along the edge of the field. The path heads down towards the Nadder valley, gradually becoming more sunken. Either side of you are banks of grass and scrub. Further down, on the northern outskirts of Barford St Martin, a housing estate comes into view. When you reach the houses, turn right and go down to join Dairy Road. Pass through the railway arch and at the junction bear left to follow the B3089 through the village. The Nadder runs parallel to the road, just a few yards away. Note Mill House on the right, with the sight and sound of the spectacular thundering mill race capturing the attention for a few moments. Pass the village school and the church. Beyond them is the Barford Inn on the left.

㉗ Lower Woodford
The Wheatsheaf

The Wheatsheaf was once a farm and what are now the dining rooms used to be the stables and barns. Various rustic artefacts characterising those pioneering days of agricultural husbandry remain. Beer was brewed here until the beginning of this century. Naturally, the inn has changed significantly over the years and today it is a thriving and friendly country pub with a good reputation for cask conditioned beers and cuisine, the accent being very much on homemade food cooked to individual requirements. One of the inn's more unusual features is an indoor fish pond and miniature footbridge dividing the dining areas. The lounge bar has a cosy fireplace and a range of cushioned bench seats. In summer you can eat and drink in the large beer garden.

There is an extensive menu and a range of chef's daily specials. Starters include soup of the day, smoked salmon, avocado Maryland and chicken liver pâté. There are delicious open sandwiches on granary bread, with a fresh crisp salad. Ploughman's incorporate West Country farmhouse cheddar and Wiltshire ham. Salads include smoked trout, tuna fish and egg, and North Atlantic prawns. Among the savoury snack dishes are lasagne verdi, chicken curry and sausage and chips. Main courses include sirloin steak, veal cordon bleu and rainbow trout. There is a good choice of vegetarian dishes, children's meals and desserts. Real ale enthusiasts won't be disappointed either. The choice includes Tanglefoot Strong Ale and Badger Best Bitter, the traditional ale brewed since 1777. Families are very welcome and children can join you in the dining area. Reservations can be taken for parties of four or more, except for Sunday and bank holiday lunchtimes.

Telephone: Middle Woodford (072273) 203.

How to get there: Lower Woodford is north of Salisbury, between the A360 and the A345. From Amesbury follow the road south through the Avon valley. From the south you can go through Wilton or Old Sarum to reach the village.

Parking: There is usually plenty of room at the Wheatsheaf, and limited spaces in the main street of Lower Woodford.

Length of the walk: 3 miles. Map: OS Landranger 184 Salisbury and the Plain (GR 124348).

The village of Lower Woodford is part of an agricultural district heavily populated with tenant farmers and landowners. William Cobbett came this way in 1826 and, remarking on the plight of the farm labourer, he expressed his 'deep shame, as an Englishman, at beholding the general extreme poverty of those who cause this vale to produce such quantities of food and raiment.'

With the sun sparkling on the Avon, bathing the watermeadows and the entire valley in a warm golden glow, Lower Woodford's unspoilt rural setting has to be one of the loveliest in the whole of Wiltshire. Appropriately, the only real way to explore the valley and appreciate its gentle beauty is to go on foot. The walk explores the windswept downland slopes to the east of the Avon before descending to Little Durnford Manor. The estate is one of the finest in the area. From here the route is across the fields back to Lower Woodford.

The Walk

From the car park turn left and pass the front of the inn. Proceed along the main street of the village, which includes various flint and brick cottages and some chalk cob walls. Soon after a telephone box on the right, you will see a footpath sign. Turn right into the drive of a private house, veering left immediately. Pass the front door of the house and continue ahead to join a path which crosses the Avon at a particularly scenic reach of the wide river. Not far from this spot are Heale House and gardens. Charles II sought refuge here after the Battle of Worcester in 1651. It was from the house that he set out to visit

114

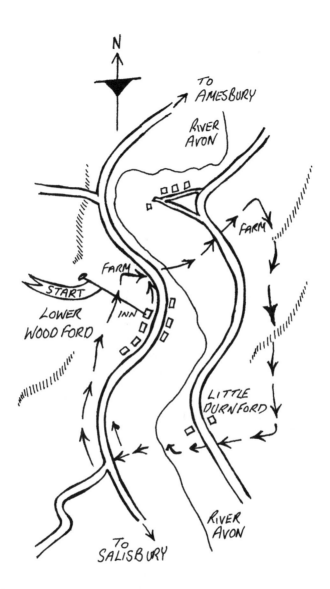

Stonehenge.

Follow the tarmac path and further up there are glorious views back across the Avon valley and the wooded downs beyond. Head up towards a farm and some cottages. At the road bear left for a few yards, then right at Salterton Farm. Take the track running up the hill away from the farm buildings. Follow it round to the right and after about 120 yards, turn right through a gate to join a path cutting along the right edge of the field. Follow the grassy strip with delightful views of the valley and Lower Woodford nestling beside the clear river and the pretty watermeadows. Eventually you reach the field corner. Go through a wooden gate, at once crossing the route of a bridleway, and continue along the waymarked footpath through a copse. Beyond it head out over open ground on the higher slopes of the valley. Follow the broad grassy ride as it descends towards some trees. Pass alongside an isolated thatched cottage and bear right just beyond it to join a quiet lane running between rows of trees. Further on, there is more extensive woodland on the right. Stay on the lane to reach a junction. Cross the road and go through a wooden panelled gate marked 'Footpath'. Follow the tarmac drive with a low flint wall and hedge on the right. Above the hedge can be glimpsed the lovely old manor house at Little Durnford. The house was the subject of a book called *A Wiltshire Home*, written by a member of the Devenish family, who lived there as a child early this century.

During late winter clusters of snowdrops are often visible over among the trees and shrubs to the right of the drive. As you approach some cottages and a stable block, veer right by a petrol pump and follow the drive towards the stone bridge over the Avon. If you look behind you at this stage, you will be able to spot the main house across the extensive lawns. At the next bridge take the path on the right. Walk across the pasture with the brook on your left. At the next bridge cross over to a stile, bear right beside the brook into the adjoining field and walk along its left edge. The brook is now on your right. Soon you reach a gate on the left. Pass through it to join a wooded track running to the road. (If there is any problem over access in these fields, follow the main drive to the road and then bear right. Follow the road as it runs past the entrance to 'The Bays' and then take a waymarked path in the left bank.)

Cross over to the signposted path. In the field head obliquely right. The path is not clear at this point; the easiest thing is to aim for the left hand edge of a line of trees. Cross a track and now the trees are a short distance away. Proceed towards them and join a path running along a field edge with some trees on the immediate right. Farm buildings are visible in the distance. The houses of Lower Woodford come into view on the right. Cross a stile and continue towards the farm. Go through a field gate in the next boundary and make for some cottages to the right of the farm buildings. There are good views on the right of Lower Woodford sheltering in the valley. At the farm gate turn right and go down the hill to the junction. Bear right and follow the road back to the inn car park.

Amesbury
The New Inn

28

Originally a coaching inn, the New Inn is, according to a written account of its history available in the bar, 'recorded in the 18th century as the Three Tuns and run by one Widow Vincent. The car park, originally a tenement garden, became, around the turn of the century, the tanyard and works of the Sandell family who continued a trade that had existed since the 14th century. Their shop was directly opposite.' Improvements have made the New Inn a smart, bright and bustling pub. It retains the feel of a friendly village inn rather than that of the town pub that it is. There is some pine panelling, various exposed beams, wall lights, part brick and stone walls. The separate dining area is small and quite intimate.

Food, which is available every day except Sunday evenings in winter, includes various sandwiches – tuna fish, prawn, traditional ham, and mature cheddar among them. There are also toasties, ploughman's, baps and jacket potatoes. Starters include chef's soup of the day and the New Inn seafood selection. T-bone steak, mixed grill, beef carbonnade (their own recipe), scampi, fillet of plaice and traditional steak and kidney pie are featured among the main courses. There is also a range of vegetarian dishes and salads, plus 'kiddies'

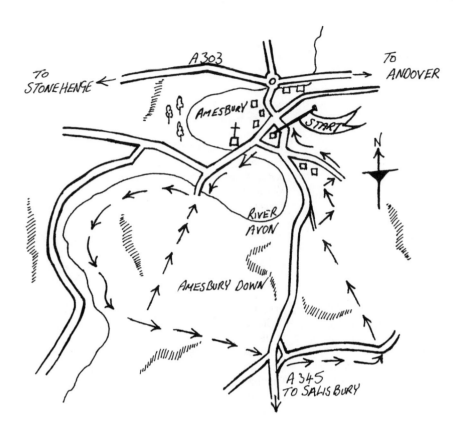

bites' and desserts. Real ales include Bunces, from Netheravon nearby, and Wadworth 6X. There is also Heineken, Stella Artois and chilled Liebfraumilch. Children are welcome, but dogs must remain outside. Telephone: Amesbury (0980) 622110.

How to get there: Amesbury is 8 miles north of Salisbury and 20 miles south of Marlborough, at the junction of the A303 and the A345. The New Inn is in High Street. Follow the signs for the town centre and bear right at the junction with Church Street. The New Inn is on the right.

Parking: There is a small car park at the side of the inn. Apart from roadside parking, Amesbury has several car parks including one in Church Street just a few yards from the inn, and a large one on the A345, near the old Plaza Cinema.

Length of the walk: 4½ miles. Map: OS Landranger 184 Salisbury and the Plain (GR 154415).

Although this entire area is rich in archaeological heritage, Amesbury is probably most closely associated with Stonehenge, a mile or two to the west of the town. This walk, however, explores the fine, lesser-known downland to the south of Amesbury, initially running parallel to the pretty waters of the river Avon before climbing over bracing Amesbury Down to the edge of RAF Boscombe Down. The final leg provides superb views of Amesbury nestling in the valley below. Much of the walk is over exposed ground, so be well wrapped up in wet or windy weather. A dry, still day with good visibility is the ideal time. When I did this walk, it was a bright, sunny morning in winter and, with the added inducement of a hard frost, it was a most memorable experience!

The walk includes a ten minute stretch along a fairly busy road carrying mainly local traffic. A suggested alternative route back to Amesbury cuts out the road but reduces the overall length of the walk by about 2 miles.

The Walk

From the New Inn car park, turn left and then at the junction go straight ahead into Church Street. Situated on the eastern fringes of Salisbury Plain, Amesbury is renowned in some quarters for its Arthurian connections as King Arthur was supposed to have possessed a fondness for this area. There are claims that the name 'Amesbury' is derived from Ambrosius Aurelianus, a Roman Briton who happened to be the uncle of King Arthur. After the King's death, in the 6th century, Queen Guinevere sought refuge at the abbey in Amesbury, and later became its abbess. An abbey remains here to this day, rebuilt in 1840.

Pass the Antrobus Arms Hotel on the left, then Amesbury church and the entrance to the abbey on the right. Follow the road down to the right hand bend, crossing over the Avon at a picturesque stretch of the river. Go forward into Recreation Road at the point where the main road becomes Stonehenge Road. Pass a cemetery on the left. As you approach the parking area in the corner of the recreation ground, veer right onto a path with woodland on the right. Cross the Avon by several footbridges. This is a particularly pleasant stretch of the walk, with the gentle river flowing between the trees.

At the junction of paths, turn right (signposted 'Normanton'). Follow the field boundary with the river a few yards away to the right through the trees. At the end of the trees, cross a stile and continue. Go over several more stiles and then a track. Keep along the field boundary, following the path as waymarked. Note the good views of the downland ridge up ahead. Soon a charming thatched cottage comes into view, nestling among the trees at the foot of the hillside. The Avon is still clearly visible at this stage of the walk.

Follow the path as it curves round to the left in the field corner. Pass through a gateway with an accompanying stile. The route is well waymarked at this point. Go through another gateway and continue along the field boundary with glimpses of watermeadows over to the right. On reaching the end of the trees on the right, follow the track round to the right. After a few yards, pass over a stile and then bear left, ignoring the waymarked Stonehenge Walk.

Proceed up the edge of the field, keeping the fence on the left. Further up, it is worth pausing to glance back towards a long line of trees on the far horizon. Ascend the slope as far as the gate. At this point you have a choice.

To avoid any road walking, turn left and follow the bridleway over the downs (signposted 'Amesbury'). After little more than ½ mile, you reach the Avon. Cross it and continue alongside the recreation ground. At the road junction, go straight ahead and back into Amesbury.

The main walk, however, continues ahead at this point, following the bridleway (White Railings, 1½ miles). Keep to the main track as it cuts across the downs to some barns and a wind-pump generator. Continue ahead over Amesbury Down, keeping the fence on your immediate right. Follow the path as it curves right and then left. The distant sound of traffic on the A345 gradually becomes audible.

Pass into the next field, with the road up ahead. In the far right corner, at the foot of the embankment, go through a wooden gate and then turn right. At the top of the bank, cross the main A345, taking great care, and make for Stockport Road (signposted 'Boscombe Down'). The next ten minutes or so involves walking on the road linking the A345 with Bulford and Boscombe Down. Pass some industrial units on the right and, when the road bends left, swing left to join a concrete farm track and follow it down to the farm buildings. There are splendid downland views along this stretch. Proceed to the right of the buildings and continue along the track. Pass through a gate and follow the byway over this high ground towards the outskirts of Amesbury. Eventually, in the field corner, you join a path running between fences and hedges. Descend the hillside, noting the spectacular views of Amesbury and its abbey lying below you in the valley of the Avon.

Further down, with houses on the right, join a tarmac path and follow it down to the one way street on the right. Turn right and follow the road as it bends left through the housing estate. Ignore Lynchfield Road and continue down to the junction. Turn right and at the junction with Earls Court Road and Boscombe Road bear left and head back into Amesbury. Cross the A345 by the old Plaza Cinema and return to the town centre

29 West Dean
The Red Lion

The Wiltshire/Hampshire county boundary runs directly through the bar, dividing the pub into two equal parts. Over the years this geographical quirk has prompted many jokes and much laughter, and in recent times, of course, wisecracks about the pub's community charge have been all the fashion! The inn occupies a charming setting in the centre of this pretty village. On summer evenings the green at the front becomes very busy. At the rear is an extensive, 5-acre area of land where children can play in safety. The field and the listed barn next door to the pub are available for functions. Inside the Red Lion, the lounge bar includes various paintings and horse brasses. There is a games room which includes a pool table, dartboard and juke box.

The Red Lion has a good selection of food including freshly made sandwiches, ploughman's – among them is the 'classic' with cheddar cheese, and a local speciality with Wiltshire ham. There are basket meals too, including cheeseburger, beefburger and chickenburger, and jumbo hotdog with pan-fried onions. A traditional Sunday roast is also available. Flowers and Wadworth 6X are the real ales and there is also a 'mystery pump'.

Telephone: Whiteparish (0794) 40469.

121

How to get there: West Dean is east of Salisbury. Coming from the city or Southampton, the most direct route is along the A36. Follow the signs for West Dean. In the village centre bear right by the green.

Parking: There is room to park at the Red Lion. The village itself offers limited spaces.

Length of the walk: 3½ miles. Map: OS Landranger 184 Salisbury and the Plain (GR 257269).

West Dean is a classic English village. It has some pretty thatched and timber framed cottages and houses, a pleasant green and a river, the Dun. At one time there were ambitious plans for a canal navigation here, linking Southampton, Salisbury and Bristol. Work on the Salisbury Canal began in 1795, but the scheme was never completed.

The walk heads for Dean Hill where there are splendid views. This is uninhabited border country, conveying a strong sense of isolation which is perhaps surprising considering its proximity to Salisbury and Southampton. The final 1½ miles is along a quiet country road.

The Walk
From the car park head for the junction, bear left over the road bridge and follow the road out of the village with the green on your left. You are heading west towards the villages of East and West Grimstead. Pass Moodys Hill on the right and continue along the road. Immediately beyond the entrance to Ordnance House on the left, go up the bank to a waymarked footpath. Follow the path along the field edge for a few yards into the next field. Bear right here and follow the right boundary. There are good views from here over to West Dean. Ahead of you the thickly wooded slopes of Dean Hill rise up to meet the skyline. Proceed towards the higher perimeter fence and turn right in the field corner over a stile. The fence on the left encloses a Ministry of Defence Armament Depot built into the side of the hill. All the familiar hallmarks of an MOD establishment are here, including military policemen patrolling with alsatians, and signs everywhere warning of the consequences of extreme behaviour!

Follow the path alongside the fence. Pass a gate into the depot and continue up the grassy hillside path. Soon the path runs up to join the road on a sharp bend. At this point there are glorious views back to the north and east. Apart from the road and the odd building, there are very few signs of humanity to be seen down in this rural border wilderness.

Join the road and follow it round the bend. The road rises quite steeply along this stretch. The views on the right across the empty

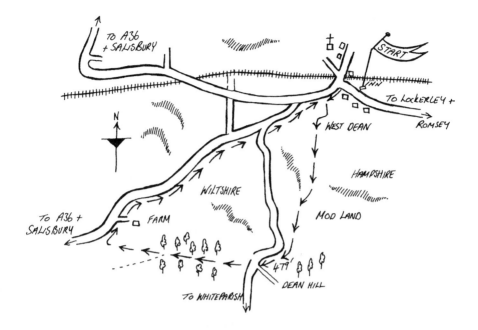

landscape are constant and unchanging. Later on, bear right to join a byway (Dean Hill Farm). Pass The White House and follow the byway between belts of woodland. When the trees thin, there are striking views again over to the right. About 100 yards beyond the woods, look for a narrow path on the right threading between gorse and brambles. Follow the chalky path as it runs parallel with the byway. Gradually it becomes more sunken, trees, undergrowth and high banks of scree closing in either side of you.

Further on, a glorious panorama to the north unfolds. Continue as far as the road and turn right. Pass a farm entrance. Over to the right along this stretch are splendid views up towards the trees of Dean Hill and the middle stages of the walk. The transmitter rises high above the hill, representing a distinctive landmark in the area. Follow the road until you reach a T junction. Bear right, back into West Dean.

③⓪ Redlynch
The King's Head

The King's Head is 17th century and very much a traditional country pub. Inside, there are some quaint old features including beams and low ceilings. Note the table mats which have old theatre and music hall bills on them. Apart from the main bar and the picture room, there is the garden room, which is open in the summer. Landlady Barbara Watkins is no ordinary publican. Some years ago she was a glamorous model much in demand. In what is known as the picture room there are various photographs of her taken at the height of her career. In other shots she can be seen posing on the decks of the Queen Mary. The strong nautical theme in the picture room is no coincidence. Barbara's late husband was a captain with Cunard for many years. There are many photographs and prints of some of the great liners, including the *Canberra, Oriana* and *Titanic. HMS Victory* and *HMS St Vincent* are also included.

The real ales on handpump are Courage Directors and Best Bitter, Ushers Best Bitter and Founders. There is a wide choice of dishes available from the menu. You can start off with homemade soup of the day and then go on to cod and chips or jumbo sausage or perhaps a ploughman's – there is cheddar, stilton or pâté. There are baked potatoes, toasted sandwiches, hot dishes including macaroni cheese, mushroom and nut fettucini or fisherman's pie. If you want something a bit more substantial, there is 6 oz prime Scotch sirloin steak and mushrooms, mixed grill and fried egg, charcoal-grilled tender half chicken or homemade steak and kidney pie, and on Sundays a roast lunch of beef or lamb. Desserts include hot chocolate fudge cake, spotted dick, bread pudding, lemon sorbet or cassata Italian ice cream. There is also a daily specials board. Children are permitted in the dining area and the garden room. There is also a garden with tables and chairs.

Telephone: Downton (0725) 20420.

How to get there: Redlynch is south of Salisbury, between the A338 and A36. At Downton join the B3080 and at Morgan's Vale bear left into Redlynch. The inn is on the left.

Parking: Apart from the car park at the King's Head, there are a few spaces near the pub or in the vicinity of Morgan's Vale.

Length of the walk: 4¼ miles. Map: OS Landranger 184 Salisbury and the Plain (GR 202213).

On the chalk downs above Redlynch there are wide, uninterrupted views over the Avon valley and north to the spire of Salisbury Cathedral. The walk explores this remote downland country, and for the naturalist there is plenty to see, including wild chalk-loving flowers and preserved hedgerows. There is an optional spur to the folly at Pepperbox Hill, increasing the route by about 1½ miles.

The Walk
Leave the car park and turn immediately right, following the quiet lane (not to be confused with the road leading up to join the B3080 at Morgan's Vale). The lane climbs up beside farmland. When you reach a triangular road junction, swing left and at the next junction veer right where there is a path opposite cutting between hedgerows. At this stage of the walk there are good views over towards the Avon valley and beyond. Pass a 'No Through Road' sign followed by several houses and bungalows. There are catkins along this stretch of the route in spring, and a sign indicating the verge is protected. Pass a field on the left sometimes inhabited by goats and continue along the track as it curves to the right. Over to the west the good views are constant.

Soon the track becomes rougher and muddier underfoot as you begin to climb up the slope. Further up, there is an old triangulation pillar in the right hand fence. Superseded by more sophisticated techniques, there have been calls to preserve these stone monuments

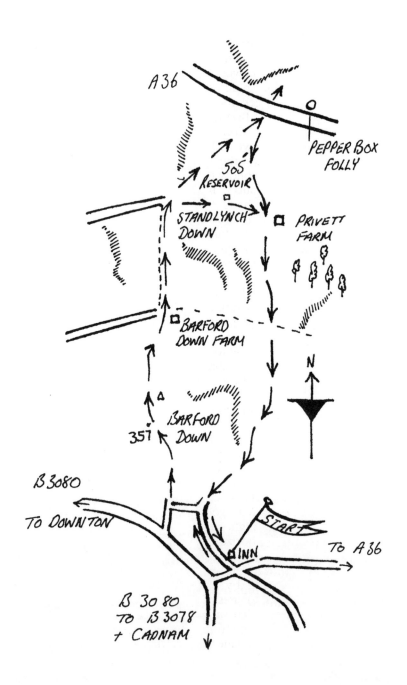

to a pre-satellite age. The pillars, of which there are many thoughout the country, were erected by the Ordnance Survey to signify an exact height. This one stands at over 350 ft above sea level. From the top there are splendid views in all directions.

Carry on down between the trees which thin somewhat as you approach the buildings of Barford Down Farm. Beyond the farm you join the road on a bend. Continue ahead along the road as it cuts across farmland. Note the westerly views. When you reach an isolated whitened brick dwelling on the left of the road, take the track on the extreme right in order to follow the main walk. Note the post box for Privett Farm which is about ½ mile away!

To extend the route as far as Pepperbox Hill, take the middle track of the three and follow it as far as the hill, crossing the busy A36 with care. The folly on top of the hill is known as the Pepperbox. In the care of the National Trust, it was built by Giles Eyre in 1606, according to legend, in order to overlook neighbouring Longford Castle. On leaving the hill retrace your steps over the road and when the track forks, take the left turning. Further on, you reach a junction. Turn left towards Privett Farm, rejoining the main route of the walk.

As you climb up the hill, pause for a few moments to admire the wonderful, far-reaching views. From here you can see the spire of Salisbury Cathedral and in the foreground the outline of 16th century Longford Castle, triangular in shape, over 2 miles away on the banks of the Avon. Glancing to the west reveals a view of Clearbury Ring, a distinctive hillfort enclosed by trees. Continue up the track passing the embankment of a small reservoir on the left. The walk becomes enclosed and altogether more sheltered now as trees close in on several sides. Just beyond the track running in from Pepperbox Hill, pass through a gate and then bear right as you approach Privett Farm. Head down the chalky track noting the views on the right over to the south west. In the banks along here grows a chalk-loving flower known as dog's mercury. Pass a crosstrack and continue between lines of trees and hedgerows. With good visibility, on the left through the gaps in the hedge you might just be able to spot the buildings of Southampton on the far horizon.

When you reach a junction of tracks, continue ahead and follow the track as it begins to curve left between hedgerows. It runs alongside farm buildings, followed by the entrance to Templeman's Old Farmhouse. The track graduates to a lane at this point. Follow its firm surface until you reach a left turning after several minutes. You will probably recognise this route from the earlier stages of the walk. Take the turning and follow the lane back to the King's Head.